NOV 18 1971

Rapid Development in Small Economies

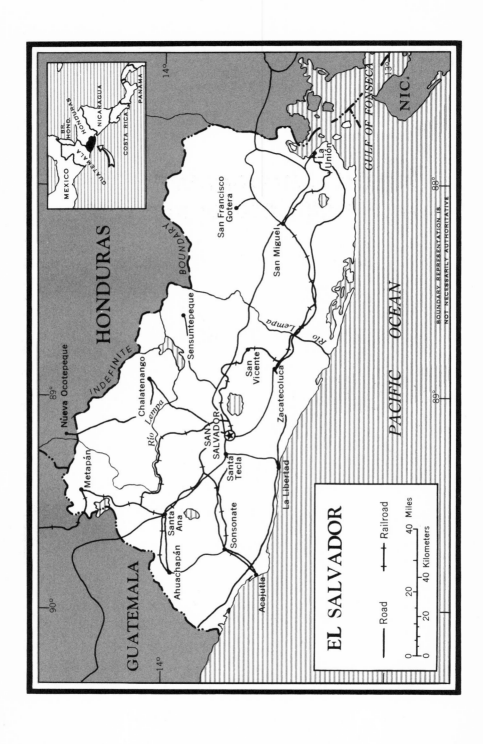

**PRAEGER SPECIAL STUDIES IN
INTERNATIONAL ECONOMICS AND DEVELOPMENT**

Rapid Development in Small Economies

THE EXAMPLE OF EL SALVADOR

David R. Raynolds

FREDERICK A. PRAEGER, Publishers
New York · Washington · London

The purpose of the Praeger Special Studies is to make specialized research monographs in U.S. and international economics and politics available to the academic, business, and government communities. For further information, write to the Special Projects Division, Frederick A. Praeger, Publishers, 111 Fourth Avenue, New York, N.Y. 10003.

FREDERICK A. PRAEGER, PUBLISHERS
111 Fourth Avenue, New York, N.Y. 10003, U.S.A.
77-79 Charlotte Street, London W.1, England

Published in the United States of America in 1967
by Frederick A. Praeger, Inc., Publishers

Library of Congress Catalog Card Number: 66-26570

Printed in the United States of America

*To my children born in El Salvador,
and to their grandparents.*

INTRODUCTION

Our wisest experts are learning that foreign aid can do most good in small countries. They are the protean economies -- the ones most readily capable of change. One of our powerful senators recognized this years ago. He told me in the early days of the Alianza that he had advised "Fowler Hamilton (the Aid Administrator) and the fellows at the State Department to stop trying to remake Brazil and to concentrate efforts where our resources and talents could do the most good." He mentioned the Dominican Republic as his candidate for our attention and assistance. I urged him to think about El Salvador. He looked over his glasses and soberly conceded that possibility. More than a year later when the Senator accompanied President Kennedy to Costa Rica for the meeting with Central American Presidents, I reminded him of our conversation and could tell him that El Salvador was already moving along towards success. It was not on the front pages, but progress was a reality.

David Raynolds' book shows why this small Republic had the elements that make for success in economic development. United States policy was willing to provide the missing components while the Salvadorans worked out their own solutions to their own national problems. That is the way of success in foreign aid. El Salvador made its own decisions. El Salvador achieved the success. The help of the United States was generous and was most effective because it did not interfere -- under the Alianza -- with the main currents of El Salvador's own national development. The United States did not impose its patterns, but could render great help in the courses that the Salvadorans had set for themselves: the development of the Central American Common Market, industrial promotion, the creation of industrial development banks, creation of new systems of credit for the small farmer, organization of savings and loan associations, and many other essentials of a growing economy.

Many nations with resources comparable to those of El Salvador have not done as well in this decade. This may have to do with the will and the determination of the Salvadorans. For a protean economy to change its shape, there must be the will to do it. Moreover, the people must be adaptable and capable of absorbing new techniques and learning modern skills. Mr. Raynolds takes perceptive note of how modern factory managers have trained Salvadoran workers for modern industry. Students of the transfer of technology can find brilliant examples of success in Salvadoran industry. These examples and the protean achievements that follow give ground for belief that the Alliance for Progress may yet prove the most successful aspect of our diplomacy in this decade.

Murat W. Williams
Former United States Ambassador
to El Salvador

Madison Mills, Virginia

PREFACE

Over two hundred years ago Adam Smith began gathering material for a classic description of economic development in a small economy. Published in 1776, The Wealth of Nations provided not only a detailed description of the British economy, but drew conclusions about economic activity in general from the British and other European examples.

Smith worked with a variety of published materials, many of which were unreliable or speculative in nature, and backed this type of research with extensive conversations, correspondence, and direct personal observation. Most economic analysis today is carried out under better circumstances, with a long chain of trained data-gatherers between the economic event and the writer in economics. This system breaks down, however, when an attempt is made to describe one of the world's smaller economies. The writer is forced to deal with elemental material, much of it little better than the kind available to Adam Smith, and direct personal observation becomes essential.

Starting in 1958, I had the good fortune to serve in the U.S. Embassy in San Salvador, El Salvador, for several years. I was soon aware that there was no general description of the development of the Salvadoran economy since the 1930's, and yet the bustle and dynamism of the economy in 1958 was in obvious contrast with the country's recent past. The men who had made possible the shift from an economy of slow, self-sufficient agriculture to one of growing industrialization were still active in affairs, and willing to explain their experiences to a foreign observer.

Detailed discussions with the participants soon showed that there was nothing smooth and inevitable about economic growth. Large aggregate figures, such as the calculations of Gross National Product, tend to obscure as much as reveal, and in a small economy they obscure the essential importance of individual decisions.

This survey does not lay much stress on political events, though I seek to describe economic change over a period of three decades. This is not because there were no political events--actually there were many dramatic changes. The period under consideration started with a bloody communist-inspired uprising known as the "sublevación," and ended with two revolutions in 1960 and 1961. Had the national economy been managed by a central government, this sort of political instability might have left no economic growth to record. This was not the case, however, and in the period under consideration the population almost doubled and production increased well over two-fold.

Because growth and progress are obvious elements in the Salvadoran economy, one is tempted to compare results with what happened in other countries. But what does one use for a basis of comparison? I soon found that comparisons with huge economies such as that of the United States had uncertain value, while comparison with neighboring Central American countries was perhaps too arbitrary and limited. Instead, I suggest that more valid comparisons can be made within the general range of economies of roughly the same population size.

A sketch of this method is provided in Chapter 12. It is not particularly elegant, because no one has gathered together extensive and comparable economic material on the more than fifty economic units in the world today which contain a population of between 1 and 6 million people. Based on my limited observation in fifteen of them, these units appear to be more comparable to each other than to the larger, massive economies. Because many of the smaller countries are developing both rapidly and with individual characteristics which do not show up from inspection of the aggregate figures, I have termed them "protean economies." This term seems helpful because, like the mythical god-man Proteus, the smaller economies still appear able to change their shapes in ways which are relatively unpredictable.

Compared with other protean economies, the growth record in El Salvador has been impressive. One would hesitate to say that any other economy with similar resources accomplished more during the period. It is quite obvious that in the last generation a number of economies on an equivalent footing accomplished less.

Printed sources of statistical material have been cited in the text, and footnotes kept to a minimum. My obligation to my many friends in El Salvador who provided me with facts about the country's development is apparent. The Department of State permitted me a brief return to private life to write this survey, and no official endorsement of the results should be implied. My wife and children steadfastly bore the throes of the gestation period. The final product remains the responsibility of the author.

D. R. R.
Lander, Wyoming 1966

CONTENTS

CHAPTER

APPENDIXES

LIST OF TABLES

CHAPTER
1   POPULATION

At some time in the decade of the 1970's, the Central American city of San Salvador will join the ranks of the world's major cities having over 1 million inhabitants. It will be the first metropolis of this size between Mexico City and Caracas. The startling growth of the capital of El Salvador is one facet of the population surge which brings both new problems and new opportunities to this rapidly developing nation. How did such growth come about? How did the country's people manage to feed, clothe, and house over a million additional citizens in less than three decades? How will they face the even larger challenges which lie ahead? A look at some of the outstanding characteristics of the population's development may supply some clues.

At the start of 1961 the population of El Salvador was about 2.5 million people. This total was almost double the population only thirty years previously. Recent studies by the national census bureau indicate the population is still growing at a rate of close to 3 percent a year, one of the highest national growth rates in the world.

This rate of population growth can be traced to several primary causes. First and foremost is a sharp decline in death rates at all age levels, brought about by recent medical advances. Two major diseases which were endemic in the area thirty years ago -- yellow fever and malaria -- have been largely eliminated by public and private health measures. The use of DDT and antibiotics has cut infant mortality rates sharply, though infant deaths still account for a sizable proportion of total deaths. Private and government hospitals, staffed by an increasing national pool of doctors and nurses, have reduced deaths from postnatal diseases and accidents.

1

While greatly improved health conditions have increased the life expectancy of the newborn, the birth rate has remained relatively stable. When the country first achieved independence in 1823, its population was about one-tenth of the current figure. Birth rates were roughly those known today. Due to high death rates then, families with only three or four children would have soon died out under nineteenth century conditions. As in other countries, the people necessarily placed high social premiums on large families. Only recently, with the drop in death rates, has any thought been given to self-imposed limitations on family size.

The improvement in health conditions is so recent that the country still has a comparatively young population. The 1950 census showed that more than 41 percent of the population was under 15 years of age. Accounts of the first Spanish explorers as well as archaeological evidence indicate that in the pre-Columbian period, less than half the population in Central America lived longer than their early teens. In the colonial period and on into the nineteenth century, grandparents were unusual. By 1950, 5 percent of the population was over the age of 60. The total number of elderly people as well as its proportion of the total population has continued to increase in the last decade.

Unlike the situation found in many countries of the Western Hemisphere, the population is racially homogeneous. Group manifestations of racial discrimination are virtually unknown. The pre-Columbian culture consisted of Indians who had some trade links with tribes in territory which later became Guatemala and Honduras. The Spanish conquerors brought with them Indian troops from their new Mexican colony, adding an Aztec strain. Later Spanish immigrants usually arrived without wives during the colonial period, leading to a rapid mixture of European with local bloodlines. In the period since independence there has been some additional immigration of people of European and Asian stock. Through the years the country remained largely a prejudice-free melting pot.

With the achievement of national independence, the country also separated church and state. While the Catholic Christian church holds the faith of the great majority of the population today, religious discrimination against other groups is seldom encountered. Lacking the historical burden of either intensive racial or religious bigotry known in other countries, recent sharp increases in population have been more equitably absorbed by the national society.

In recent years the population has become quite mobile within the country, largely due to improved transportation conditions. Agricultural pursuits, still the major source of employment, have encouraged temporary as well as permanent resettlement of agricultural workers and their families. Urban life, with its excitement as well as conveniences, has proved increasingly attractive. The sharpest urban growth has been apparent in the capital city of San Salvador, though other urban centers are showing growth trends as well.

The case of urban growth in San Salvador is particularly startling. The city was founded by the early Spanish settlers near an Indian town, in a well-watered area flanked by volcanic ridges and one active volcano. The city's size was stable in the early twentieth century, with less than 100,000 inhabitants. In 1917 a combination of earthquakes and an eruption of the neighboring volcano destroyed many of the buildings and other improvements which had survived similar disaster in the past. During the decade of the 1920's, the city added little population, but by the 1930's, rapid growth began.

By 1961, the city together with its immediate suburban areas held close to 300,000 people. The recent sharp rate of growth, which shows no signs of abatement, will produce a capital with a population of over 1 million within the next twelve to fifteen years. Greater San Salvador then will be the largest city in the Central America area, with about 25 percent of the national population.

Rural population growth, on the other hand, has been limited in the past thirty years by two principal factors: the attractions of urban living and employment noted above, and technological changes which tend to limit agricultural employment. Crop production has more than doubled in the past thirty years. Despite higher levels of production and the introduction of new labor-intensive crops such as cotton, improvements in agricultural technology have tended to dampen the demand for full-time agricultural workers. Since much of the country's agriculture is only partially mechanized, further gains in labor productivity appear to be inevitable through the next few decades and will tend to restrict expansion of the agricultural population.

The expansion potential of intermediate-sized market towns also appears to be limited. This is largely due to the country's advanced transportation network, which makes all locations generally accessible to the capital area. Industrial development is concentrating in the capital area, and no other urban location appears to have the near-term potential of a population over 100,000. Present government plans for additional transportation development suggest that the capital area will become even more accessible. The country's second largest city, Santa Ana (once more important commercially than the capital itself) appears to be stabilizing at a population of about 75,000. The eastern trade center of San Miguel has a population of under 50,000, while the three main ports of Acajutla, La Libertad, and La Unión, together with the marketing/transportation centers of Sonsonate, San Vincente, Zacatecoluca, and Usulután, are all smaller.

Population figures in themselves have meaning for economists and demographers, but for most people the individual implications underlying the figures are more tangible. A farmer in the eastern zone of the country states sadly that three of his five living sons have moved from the family homestead to nearby small towns, while a fourth is working in the capital. Only thirty years ago the rural child who left home was viewed with some suspicion, as were the comparatively few strangers who settled in the rural areas. The present loss of rural children to the small towns and larger cities, while less crushing to their parents than the separations caused by former high death rates, still makes for painful situations which the older generation finds hard to understand.

The same farmer faces another unexpected problem brought about by improved health conditions. When he grew up, the family farm supported his mother, father, two sisters and himself, or a total of five. Today his parents are still alive and live on the farm, while he and his wife have raised their five sons and three daughters. In this generation the farm has had to support twelve people instead of five. The children helped in the fields almost as soon as they could walk, and today some live independently in other towns and cities. Through this period of change, the farmer had to manage his farm far more productively than his father before him.

A school teacher points out a basic problem posed by a youthful population: in his market town, he estimates that over one-quarter of the population is in the 6 to 15 year age bracket, and hence at the prime age for education. The pressures on physical facilities and trained personnel are such that the best solution appears to be to assure universal education through the third grade level, with a resultant slighting of most of the older potential students. Since many children already work effectively by the time they are ten years old, there is also a conflicting demand for their help in the market or on the farm.

The population explosion in the capital is foreshadowing problems of unprecedented magnitude in the country's history. A highway engineer working with the Ministry of Public Works notes that the city's streets are already jammed with automobiles and trucks, and then shows on a map how much of the center of the city would have to be rebuilt to accommodate just a tripling of the vehicle population. A telephone engineer says that the national telephone system faces a major problem in laying main cables, since street and building relocations will immediately have their impact on telephone lines. Similar problems are being studied by the planning departments in the bureaus concerned with public sanitation and water. On the lighter side, a former mayor says that if the city continues to expand at its present pace, it will soon become impossible to stage a manageable parade on the main avenue due to lack of space for spectators.

Many Salvadorans who study the current population picture fear the future, because the country already has the highest population density per square mile of any nation on the mainland in the Western Hemisphere. This increasing population pressure on the land undoubtedly would present increasing problems if the country remained wholly agricultural in its economic life. On the other hand, some European countries, such as Belgium and the Netherlands, have successfully made the transition from agricultural to industrial economies, while supporting denser populations. Furthermore, many American states, such as Massachusetts (which is roughly the same size as El Salvador), support far denser populations while still providing agricultural employment to part of their labor force.

A more valid approach to population density would take into account not only the number of people in relation to area, but also the total number of people acting as a national unit. Much of the delay in the country's industrialization, for example, has been due to the limited size of the population that can act as consumers for mass production products. In an effort to overcome the restrictive effects of a small marketing target, the country has been a leader in the Central American effort to create a common market of six countries with a total of over 10 million people. Increases in El Salvador's own national population would have the same effect though on a smaller scale by increasing both producers and consumers in the economic equation.

Development of individual capabilities is in some ways encouraged by the very fact that the country at present has a small population. History has shown that some of the richest gains of the human race have been produced in relatively small national groups, such as the city states of Greece in the pre-Christian era, and the later flourishing of the Renaissance Italian city states. One of the most noticeable characteristics of the country to foreign visitors from metropolitan centers, such as New York or European capitals, is the breadth and depth of opportunity available to educated Salvadorans. Save for those in a few highly specialized occupations such as medicine, few of the country's leaders have limited themselves to a single rigidly defined profession as practiced in highly urbanized areas. Instead, a Salvadoran during his life may be an engineer and a statesman, a farmer and a banker, a scholar and an industrialist. These wide professional horizons broaden the outlook of many of the country's leaders and create the potential for sophisticated approaches to the country's problems. In the next few decades there is every reason to expect that widening education of the population will further increase this potential.

Some statistical features of the Salvadoran population are outlined in Table 1, together with some projections for the next decade.

TABLE 1

The Population of El Salvador

	1930 Census	1950 Census	1960 est.	197- est.
Total Population	1,434,400	1,855,900	2,500,000	4,000,000
Urban Population	550,500	677,400	1,100,000	1,900,000
Major cities:				
San Salvador	90,000	162,000	280,000	1,000,000
Santa Ana	40,000	51,700	70,000	100,000
San Miguel	13,000	26,700	35,000	50,000
Work Force (1/3 of population)	478,100	618,600	833,300	1,333,300

SOURCES: 1930 and 1950 figures from rounded national census data. 1960 and 197- estimates by the author.

CHAPTER 2   CLIMATE AND LAND

El Salvador has a very stable climate, without great seasonal variations in temperature. Nights tend to be a few degrees cooler than days. Extremes of heat or cold are unknown, with maximum recorded variations lying between 45° and 105° Fahrenheit. Temperature variations between locations are due more to altitude than to localized weather conditions.

Aside from its agreeable temperature, the main feature of the climate is the concentration of rainfall in the so-called "rainy season." Average national rainfall is 72 inches, and almost all occurs in the May-October period. At the height of the dry season, desert-type aridity is unknown, while rain storms lasting more than several hours in the rainy season are usually rare.

The terrain of the country shows the effects of volcanic action, both in the distant past and on up to the present. The northern frontier country is composed of a plateau punctuated by the eroded remains of extinct volcanos. The central area is dominated by a chain of more recent volcanos, some of which are not extinct. This chain begins in Guatemala, crosses the Gulf of Fonseca, and appears again in Nicaragua. In addition to volcanic effects, it is also the center of seismographic activity. From the central range, land slopes down to the Pacific coastal plain.

The central mountain chain is the site of most of the country's large centers of population, including the capital. Settlement has been encouraged by the comfortable climate, the availability of water, and rich soil produced by the gradual decomposition of lava and volcanic dust. While the average population density is about 320 people for each of the country's 8100 square miles, actual densities are much lower along the northern frontier and Pacific plain, and higher in the central range.

The country's three main lakes, Ilopango, Coatepeque, and Güija, all permit small fishery operations, but their shores are not densely settled. These and other lakes share volcanic origins. The non-volcanic lake of Zapotitán, now reduced to a small swamp, once covered a large area to the west of the capital. The former lake bed now includes some of the country's richest agricultural land.

One main river, the Lempa, dominates the country. It runs from west to east in the northwest quarter of the country, and then cuts due south in such a way that it divides the central mountain chain in half. While the river is not greatly used for navigation, it is the largest stream between the Rio Grande of Mexico and the Orinoco in Venezuela. In pre-Columbian days the lower portions of the river served as an effective territorial division between Indian tribes. Other rivers, chiefly the Rio Grande de Sonsonate in the west and the Rio Grande de San Miguel in the east, are much smaller than the Lempa. Only the Lempa has the necessary characteristics for hydro-electric power generation on an economic scale, and development of this type is being carried out rapidly.

While the land has been a bountiful source of agricultural production, its volcanic origin is not conducive to extensive mineral wealth. Sedimentary strata underlie comparatively recent volcanic deposition, but the lava shields discourage exploration for oil. There has been limited mining of some heavier minerals (gold, silver, lead, zinc), but mineralized locations are deformed by intrusive volcanic rocks which inhibit large-scale mining projects.

The future interplay of climatic and terrain conditions can be illustrated by the way they will affect future growth of San Salvador. At present the capital has a number of suburban satellite towns immediately outside the city limits. These towns (Antigua Cuscatlán, San Antonio Abad, Mejicanos, Cuscatancingo, Villa Delgado, Soyapango, Ilopango, and San Marcos) all have commuter populations working and shopping within the city limits. To the west the city of Santa Tecla (population about 30,000) has its own city life, but is becoming more closely bound to the capital each year.

Topographic limitations caused by the sharply rising hills and mountains around the capital suggest that its future development will be star-shaped, along relatively level land contours. The longest axis is taking shape along the Inter-American Highway from Santa Tecla through downtown San Salvador eastward beyond the Ilopango international airport. A second major axis is developing from Mexicanos south through the city on to San Marcos, high on the Los Planes ridge. Other main settled areas are radiating out to absorb San Antonio Abad, Cuscatancingo, Villa Delgado, and Soyapango.

Industry will tend to center along the most concentrated transportation routes. These include the right-of-way of the Inter-American Highway, noted above, and, more particularly, land in the vicinity of Ilopango, which also provides ready access to rail and air facilities. Government centers are clustered in the heart of downtown San Salvador. Higher terrain, while providing attractive housing locations, is probably less suited to industrial plants or government offices.

As the city grows to the projected magnitude of one million people in the decade of the 1970's, it will require new sources of potable and industrial water. At present these supplies come from springs replenished by rainfall, plus private wells. A major potential water resource exists in the fresh water lake of Ilopango. Present industrial development near the lake plus projected industrial and housing demand there will probably lead to employment of the lake as a major source of water for the enlarged urban area.

City growth will displace some corn, sugar, and coffee production from the immediate capital area. Local production of these crops does not bulk large in national terms, and hence the loss of the land to agricultural use will not exert a major drag on the country's output. On the contrary, the projected sharp growth of the city should encourage more intensive cultivation of land within a fifty-mile radius of the city, with some shifts from export crops to food crops for local consumption. The uniformly temperate climate will permit two and perhaps three crops a year for many types of produce.

CHAPTER

3 AGRICULTURE

A discussion of Salvadoran agriculture should distinguish the essentially different roles of crops produced for export and those grown solely for local consumption. As far back as can be traced, there has always been specialized export production in the area. In the pre-Columbian period, the local Indians traded cocoa from coastal stands for obsidian, jade, and various utensils produced outside the present national territory. Early Spanish settlers established production of Peruvian balsam (so called because it was transshipped on Peruvian galleons) on the Pacific coast. Later export interest centered in indigo, which was cultivated along the northern frontier. Export production was vital to the Spanish settlers as a source of income for their necessary imports, which ranged from horses to iron. The present division of agricultural production today still shows an export sector (coffee, cotton, sugar) and a variety of crops produced for local use.

THE EXPORT SECTOR

The bulk of the country's agricultural export production is grown on plantations (fincas) where one landowner hires permanent and temporary labor to assist in growing and harvesting. Small landholders and sharecroppers are relatively unimportant (and relatively inefficient) contributors to the export crops. The way crop lands and sales returns are distributed among the population are vital factors in determining the nature of the country's economy.

Two twentieth century examples outside El Salvador illustrate the possible extremes in land ownership, productivity, and income distribution. Some primitive tribes today still practice

11

communal agriculture under a system with minimum individual specialization and relatively equal distribution of the crops. Under this system, private land ownership does not exist. These tribes are noted for their lack of savings and exposure to extinction in times of crop failure. Without the combination of tribal savings and individual specialization, they have been unable to develop some of the rudiments of civilization, such as an alphabet.

The opposite extreme from communal ownership is monopoly ownership of the land and its fruits, as currently practiced by the Communist regimes of Russia and Red China. In an effort to wring out savings for industrialization or other party purposes, such as warfare, the ruling party hierarchy has maintained the wages of agricultural labor at minimum levels. In periods of extreme repression the regimes have deliberately killed millions of their agricultural workers through individual executions or state-sponsored starvation. The Communist method is more productive than that of the primitive tribe, but includes a far higher toll in human suffering.

In El Salvador, as in most countries, the citizens have avoided these extremes. Plantation profits not needed for immediate consumption have been invested in other projects. The effect of these savings has been most apparent in recent industrial, transportation, and electric power development. Agricultural wages are low, with savings concentrating in the hands of plantation owners. It is difficult to discern how the Salvadorans could have financed their rapid development in the past three decades without drawing savings from agriculture. Citizens are not yet in full agreement, however, whether it is more preferable to have agricultural savings concentrated in the hands of private enterpreneurs or under the direct control of a stronger central government.

Coffee

A detailed United Nations study in the mid-1950's indicated that about two hours of Salvadoran labor go into the production of each pound of green coffee delivered at dockside. At present, Salvadoran coffee sells in international markets at around $0.40 per pound. In recent years, income from the international sale of coffee was the main source for the economic development of the country. Paradoxically, the need for an intensive use of human labor in its production shows that for most Salvadorans, coffee must be a poor man's crop.

Coffee production began in El Salvador about a century ago, while most export farmers were still interested in indigo production. The introduction of an alternate source of foreign income was fortunate, since the development of dye substitutes after the turn of the century totally destroyed the world indigo market. By the end of World War I, coffee had become the major source of foreign exchange.

In the decade of the 1930's, the world-wide depression sharply reduced international coffee prices. World War II brought about a rise, and the removal of price controls in the United States brought about further increases after the war. Following price controls during the Korean War, world prices shot to record highs in the period 1956-57. Present prices are nearer the levels prevailing during the early 1950's.

The price shifts took place because of factors largely beyond the control of Salvadoran coffee farmers. While the country is the third largest producer in the Western Hemisphere, its total share of world coffee trade is far overshadowed by the massive crops of Brazil, Colombia, and some African areas. Leaders of the national coffee industry as well as the central government have been active participants in recent world coffee agreements designed to stabilize prices, but they cannot ignore the potential risks of further international declines in the price of their main source of foreign exchange. Augmented production alone would not compensate for declining prices--particularly if other major producers increased crops as well. The present volume of coffee production is about double that in the 1930's, with 70 percent of the increase taking place after World War II. In the last several years, however, there has been less interest in adding to coffee plantations.

Most Salvadoran coffee is grown on volcanic mountainsides, usually under the shade of larger trees. Young coffee plants become producing bushes within five years, and then remain efficient producers for many decades. After caring for the young plants, cultivation includes fertilizing the trees and pruning branches which are either malformed or growing too high for easy picking. Picking is concentrated in the months of October-February, depending on location. It involves the hand selection of ripe coffee cherries, with each tree picked two or three times as the cherries reach the proper maturity. The cherries are then carried quickly to a coffee processing center or beneficio. Here an extensive washing in warm water induces fermentation in the cherry, splitting it and disclosing the twin coffee beans inside. These wet beans are sun-dried in large open patios. Then, in a milling operation, the thin parchment husk of each bean is removed. The green milled beans are finally hand-graded and sacked for export according to strict brand standards.

The Salvadoran coffee industry enjoys a world-wide reputation for efficiency. Yet in the steps outlined above, it will be noted that there is extensive use of hand labor. Many growers have experimented with varying methods to improve production, but have found few alternatives tending to substitute mechanical for human labor. Limited productivity gains appear to be possible in fertilization of the trees and in transportation of the cherries to the beneficio. Larger gains in productivity may be possible at the beneficios themselves. One operator, who already has a highly mechanized beneficio, has assisted in the development of small light tractors for turning the beans in the large sun-drying patios between the washing and hulling operations. Others have experimented with chemical additives in the washing-fermentation process. Machines have been developed in the United States which can sort and grade coffee beans by size, shape, and color, but it is not known whether such installations would merit their capital costs except at the largest beneficios.

The ownership pattern in the various phases of the coffee industry has given rise to some dissatisfaction in the country. The crop occupies more than one fifth of the national land under cultivation, not including pastures and forests. Four percent of the country's growers control almost 60 percent of the coffee land, and account for nearly three quarters of the national coffee production. Many of the large land holdings consist of the sum of widely scattered coffee fincas. A somewhat more even distribution of coffee land ownership might be achieved through sale to small holders. Extreme partition of coffee land, however, would probably lead to inefficiencies in production. Under present conditions a shortage of national agricultural labor at crop time is offset by the temporary migration of tens of thousands each year from nearby Honduras and Guatemala. Division into very small holdings would complicate picking problems and probably lead to considerable spoilage.

The beneficios are centrally located in the major producing areas. Beneficio owners often have producing lands themselves, and process both their own coffee and that of their neighbors. The country's largest beneficio, for example, handles the large production of its owners and the coffee of over 4,000 other growers. In addition to treating the coffee itself, the beneficios also funnel crop loans to smaller growers. These loans are advanced during the growing period, and are paid off in cash or through consignment sales of processed coffee.

At the export stage, operations are carried out by firms of varying sizes, some of which are owned by people with interests in fincas and beneficios as well. Sales are negotiated within the framework of regulations set forth by producer organizations, a semi-autonomous national coffee board, and the terms of international coffee marketing agreements to which El Salvador is a party. The major markets are the United States and West Germany, with Germany recently taking as much coffee as the traditional American market. German retail methods put premiums on carefully selected beans with good bin appearance, since housewives buy their coffee in bean form. In the United States and other markets, the final purchaser usually gets his coffee roasted and ground, and hence appearance is less important. In recent years German prices have been higher than those in New York for comparable grades, encouraging the current realignment of exports.

Despite the high concentration of coffee land ownership at the base of the productive process, at each stage (finca, beneficio, and exporter) there are many participants whose interests conflict with those of the other stages. The national government enters as a major participant as the coffee is exported. It levies a tax on coffee exports which is progressively larger as prices increase. Since the coffee tax is one of the largest single sources of governmental revenue, the government tends to be more concerned with the level of prices and export volume than in how the proceeds from export sales are distributed within the three stages of the production/ sales process.

The paradox of highly concentrated profits and low wage levels remains, however, to perplex the entrepreneurs who have built industries with their coffee earnings. A young manufacturer of a medium-cost consumer product points out that his own employees on his finca seldom buy his product. If he raised wages to the point that he no longer had any finca earnings, he could not expect that the net increase in wages would be spent on his industrial production alone. Rather, it would be spent for a range of things from food to imported consumer goods. At present he needs some finca profits to carry inventory at his factory, even though it is operating considerably below its designed capacity. He also notes that the wholesale value of his coffee production has been cut in half in the past several years. His solution to this dilemma has been to raise the wages of his most productive workers in cautious stages, hoping that he (and other industrialists who find themselves in the same position) will gradually recoup the additional outlay through increased industrial sales.

The industrialization process means that the value of Salvadoran labor will gradually increase as industrial workers become more productive per hour than their farming counterparts. Increased labor productivity in turn usually leads to widening wage differentials. If carried on for several decades, the cost of employing a Salvadoran will become sufficiently high so that a low-productivity industry like coffee (with the two hours of labor input for a $0.40 product) will become increasingly uneconomic. This trend will result in two major changes from the present situation: coffee production will be less attractive, and the country will have to develop other sources of export income.

As previously noted, most coffee is grown on the volcanic mountainsides in the country. This terrain is not suitable for row crops, but agricultural replacements could be developed in other tree crops, particularly fruit production. The gathering and marketing of fruit is less labor intensive than coffee, suggesting that orchards could be operated by small holders rather than as plantations. Fruit trees also tend to produce more gross value per year than coffee trees, so the shift may also provide direct economic gain. In addition to diversion to orchard crops, other coffee land may eventually become utilized as housing sites or as park areas.

Cotton

A minor amount of cotton was grown in El Salvador in the early 1930's. It was locally processed and then used in small textile mills and for home handicrafts. Since World War II, the acreage under cotton went up fivefold and production is fifteen times greater. Local demand, though much larger than in the prewar period, now accounts for only about 15 percent of present production, with the rest shipped abroad.

The spectacular rise in cotton production can be traced to several causes. Most important were the medical/chemical advances in recent years. Medical improvements checked the ravages of maleria and yellow fever along the country's coastal plain. Previously this land was largely unfarmed, or used as grazing grounds for cattle. Once the land became safe for year-around habitation, intensive agriculture became feasible. The development of DDT and other insecticides supplemented medical breakthroughs by permitting the economic elimination of insect devastation, formerly the scourge of any densely cultivated row crop in the lowlands.

In the immediate postwar period, international pent-up demand for cotton textiles was quickly reflected in rising cotton prices. United States agricultural policy had the effect of putting a floor under the increased world prices. Salvadoran entrepreneurs discovered that cheap land was available which, combined with modest investments in equipment, would produce high profits with only limited market risk.

In 1940, cotton producers formed a cotton cooperative which became a centralized source for technical assistance. In addition to providing crop advice, the cooperative acts as a centralized buying agent for fertilizers and insecticides, rents crop-dusting airplanes to its members, and owns cotton gins. It also has quasi-governmental functions through its ability to pass on planting applications. Once the national crop is ginned, the cooperative stores and sells it to the local and international markets. It also operates as a credit agency during the year, advancing funds which it obtains from local banks.

Though the traditions of the cotton industry are new, it is already highly efficient in terms of land utilization. Yields per acre are equal to those obtained on irrigated acreage in the United States.   Close attention to seed selection and cultivation procedures has led to the production of high-grade fiber.   With its reputation well-established internationally, export problems have been reduced. Most of the crop now goes to Japan each year.

The pay of cottonfield workers is at about the level of coffee wages and considerably below industrial wages. This low wage level in part reflects limited worker productivity, which may increase in future years with increased mechanization. As in the case of coffee (and also sugar), the main demand for labor comes at picking time. Unlike the coffee case, additional mechanization of cotton picking is clearly possible.

Sugar

Plantation farming of sugar was introduced by the Spanish settlers in the early days of the colony, both to provide for local needs and for export.   Economic production requires flat land with favorable soil and water conditions.   Experience showed that the plots of land chosen by the original Indian settlers for their corn growing communities were ideal for sugar production.   Through the years sugar has replaced corn production in these highly favored locations.

By the 1930's, sugar was being produced at a level to fill national needs and provide a small export surplus. Internal consumption was low due to the limited size of the population and its low purchasing power.   Most of the cane was processed into a crude form (panela) which is somewhat like brown sugar and is sold in chunks about the size of a fist.   Some sulphite mills produced a coarse white sugar for premium consumption.

In the postwar period demand rose quickly, chiefly for white sugar.   Sugar output more than doubled in the last decade, though land in cultivation actually declined a modest amount.   The output gains were largely due to increased efficiency at the growing stage, and the construction of more favorably situated grinding mills. In addition to the 21 grinding mills now in operation, a modern refinery started up in 1960.

Unlike the current situation in coffee and cotton production, important labor savings appear possible in sugar production.   Ground preparation, as in the case of cotton, can be highly mechanized.   Planting and weeding also provide some opportunities for machine use.   The major productivity gains, however, appear possible in harvesting the sugar, transporting it to the mill, and in the milling process itself. At present the cane is cut by individuals using machetes, then loaded by hand into oxcarts, and driven to the mills. About 60 percent of the cane land still sends its produce to small grinders (trapiches), where the cane is ground with a small motor or by ox-power to produce panela.   The introduction of motorized cutting and transport would save labor at the first stages, while the construction of additional sulphite grinding mills would upgrade the resulting product from the lower-valued panela.   In combination, these changes might reduce local prices for raw sugar, which are more than double those in the world market.   Cane yields can also be further increased by more intensive irrigation, which at present is employed on about 10 percent of the sugar land.

About 20 percent of Salvadoran sugar production is exported each year, mostly to neighboring Honduras.   This is in contrast to the coffee and cotton crops, where the bulk of output goes abroad.   It is possible that local marketing regulations and price controls on sugar have postponed the possible gains in efficiencies outlined above.   In any event, if production is to be increased for export markets, the industry must become more efficient to match present conditions in other exporting countries.

Summary

In summarizing the country's recent experience with its main agricultural exports, several salient features should be stressed.   Each of these crops appears to require plantation-type farming to be most productive--not only in El Salvador, but in other countries as well.   Plantations at present rely on abundant supplies of low-cost human labor, particularly at harvesting time.   National concentration on coffee, cotton, and sugar exports necessarily puts the country into direct competition with any other part of the world where warm land and abundant labor supplies exist.   As we look into the future, it is hard to see how El Salvador can compete for many decades in world export markets with these particular crops, unless the people are willing to keep plantation wages and living standards low.

Already the three products are in world oversupply, with downward price tendencies. The country's hope to increase foreign exchange earnings would be enhanced by shifts to other products on this score alone. Meanwhile, other countries less advanced on the road to industrial development will probably increase their production of these crops as an initial way to earn international funds.

Productive efficiency in these three crops appears to decline as landholdings drop to family-sized units. Yet in El Salvador there is strong pressure for a more even distribution of landholdings. If holdings are subdivided, some indicated production drops may be overcome by increased managerial and mechanical efficiency, as well as the conversion of more favorable land into small holdings. Some production drops still would appear inevitable, however, due to the nature of the crops themselves and their intensive labor requirements at certain periods of the crop cycle. If public policy dictates decreased production in these crops as a necessary side effect of land reform measures, another strong argument is provided for additional crop diversification.

The evidence of the last decade testifies to the ability of Salvadoran farmers to develop increases in production per acre in the export crops. By international yardsticks, present yields appear high in coffee and cotton, while further gains in yields appear possible in sugar. The limited evidence available does not suggest that employment in these three crops has risen as rapidly as production, indicating a rise in labor and capital productivity as well. These favorable developments, summarized below in Table 2, suggest that the country may be able to engage in further diversification with some confidence.

TABLE 2
Export Crop Production and Yields*

Crop	Annual Average 1951-5		Annual Average 1956-60		1960/1 Yield 1951-5=100
	Area	Production	Area	Production	
Coffee	11.4	15	11.6	19	132
Cotton	2.3	3	4.8	7	108
Sugar	1.3	6	1.4	10	174

*Area in 10,000 hectares; production in 100,000 quintales.

SOURCE: Banco Central de Reserva, Revista Mensual.

DOMESTIC CROPS

Corn

Since pre-Columbian times, corn has been the mainstay of the national diet. Many food supplements have been added in recent times, but today the average per capita consumption of corn is somewhere between 160 and 180 pounds each year.

Corn is grown by about 230,000 farmers on a total land area of 220,000 manzanas (1 manzana = 1.73 acres). As noted previously, some formerly productive corn land is now planted in sugar and cotton. Present methods yield about 15 quintales (1 quintal = 101.4 pounds) per manzana on average each year. A fair amount of acreage produces two crops, and in exceptional cases, three crops a year.

Despite the central position of corn in the national diet, the country must import about one quarter of its present needs each year. The imports come from neighboring Central American countries (chiefly Honduras) and occasionally from the United States. The chronic shortfall in production has its chief cause in the limited use of modern growing techniques. This is quite unlike the situation in coffee, cotton, and sugar, where international competition increasingly has encouraged and forced high levels of productivity. In contrast, Salvadoran corn producers have been shielded from outside competition by the fact of national scarcity, coupled with strict import controls.

In its most primitive applications, corn technology is little advanced from that used by the pre-Columbian Indians. Toward the close of the dry season, brush or last year's corn stubble is burned in place. "Fire agriculture," particularly at this time of year, is a direct invitation to erosion, initially from dust storms and later from the first spring rains. Many denuded hillsides testify to the permanent damage which this practice has caused in the last few decades.

After clearing, the soil may be plowed or, under the most primitive methods, the sod is pierced with a digging stick. Corn seed is planted after the first week of rains, perhaps with beans or squash planted between the corn rows. Two or three weedings usually represent the maximum investment of energy before the crop matures.

When the major crop ripens toward the close of the rainy season, the farmer bends each ear downward on the stalk. The purpose of leaving corn in the field is to avoid rodent and insect damage which would normally occur if the ears were stored in one unprotected location. After the rains, corn left on the stalk can dry slowly with a minimum of fermentation. Picking for home or market use is usually postponed until the corn is actually wanted.

Small landholders growing corn on this basis need not work intensively on their crop. This permits them to hire out as harvest hands at nearby plantations producing the major export crops. Many small growers have enough corn production for family needs, and rely on the seasonal harvesting employment for cash income. Most of the landholdings in corn are little larger than that needed to produce enough for a family of five--or roughly half a manzana.

Because corn is such a vital crop, the government has sought to stabilize its price at $4.00 per quintal. This price has been selected to give the farmer adequate rewards, while protecting the city dwellers from disastrous price fluctuations which occurred several times in the 1930's and 1940's. A board which operates granaries supervises this price structure, and also regulates the importation of corn to supplement national production.

Even at the $4.00 corn price, farmers have learned that where possible, a shift from corn into coffee, cotton, or sugar brings more profitable production per unit of land. This fact, combined with the limited availability of crop land in the country, would at first appear to present bleak prospects for expanding national corn production.

Fortunately, fully proven technological developments are gradually being introduced which will revolutionize Salvadoran corn production and bring striking side effects in rural areas. The major breakthrough has been the development of suitable hybrid corn strains for the tropics through research carried out by the Rockefeller Foundation, other private groups, and the U.S. International Cooperation Agency.* Hybrid production in El Salvador, under a variety of conditions, has shown

---

*The International Cooperation Agency (ICA) is now known as the Agency for International Development (AID).

average yields of 50 to 70 quintales per manzana, a very large jump from the 15 quintal per manzana yield of native strains. Hybrid corn can be grown with the same primitive techniques usually employed. Thus a farmer who merely changes his type of seed can triple production with little additional effort. Even better results are obtained if modest amounts of fertilizer are used.

A small farmer living northwest of Santa Ana illustrates what the shift from native to hybrid corn can mean. On his sloping hillside holding of about one manzana, he formerly produced about 15 quintales, or the national average. He, his wife, and three small children ate about 8 quintales each year. His wife sold the remaining 7 quintales in a small market town, bringing in a cash income of $28 a year. This amount was important to them, and was about equal to piece-work wages for a month's coffee picking by the husband.

When the farmer shifted to hybrid corn, he obtained the new seed free as a demonstration project for the Ministry of Agriculture. He followed his normal field routine, but at crop time he had 60 quintales of corn. Subtracting family needs of 8 quintales, his wife now had corn worth $208 for local marketing. In effect, this shift brought about a seven-fold increase in family income for some extra labor in harvesting. The income gained was more than both husband and wife could earn during a three-month coffee harvest. Since this experience, the farmer has been buying hybrid seed, experimenting in the use of natural and chemical fertilizers, and is saving money to buy more land.

Despite the striking gains possible, the country will not shift over to hybrid production overnight. Custom stands in the way on three counts. Farmers themselves are suspicious of hybrid corn because the kernels are not suitable for re-planting. This suspicion has been transmitted to town and city customers, who reason by analogy that eating hybrid corn will act as a detriment to their virility. Furthermore, those cooking hybrid corn note that it has different behavior during preparation than the native varieties. Time will demolish these negative arguments as more farmers seek increased income, consumers observe the unchecked rise in national population, and housewives make small changes in food preparation.

In many locations along the northern frontier, once the heart of the indigo-producing region, corn production has been dropping for years due to increasing erosion and mineral losses in the soil. Normal applications of fertilizer in test plots failed to restore anticipated yields. A chance combination of fertilizers in a demonstration area used by the Ministry of Agriculture and the International Cooperation Administration brought another breakthrough: an almost catalytic soil reaction which unlocked the nutrients in commercial fertilizers. Farmers in this region now can increase the yields of native corn by employing fertilizer, as well as bring formerly discarded lands back into production. Even larger benefits can be obtained by a shift to hybrid strains.

Mechanical improvements in handling the corn crop may prove more difficult to introduce widely than innovations in the use of seed and fertilizers. Small holdings of one manzana or so can not produce enough to justify the investment in heavy tools. Furthermore, the sloping terrain worked by many farmers rules out self-propelled equipment. Farmers facing these limitations but shifting to higher yielding hybrid corn can divert part of their increased income to the purchase of steel hoes, plows, and draft animals. Alternative methods also must be employed to replace the presently wasteful method of "fire agriculture" in clearing the fields, since this is particularly destructive of sloping land.

On larger, more level landholdings, corn production can become fully mechanized. Tractor plowing, fertilizing, seeding, weeding, and harvesting are all well-developed techniques. Farmers with suitable land can hope to emulate methods developed in the corn belt of the United States, where one household with mechanical assistance can crop the equivalent of more than 100 manzanas of corn. Production of this magnitude will require that care be taken to construct secure on-farm storage facilities for the crop. Larger farmers can also supplement their incomes by harvesting the cornstalks for use as cattle feed.

The factors outlined above suggest that at present price levels, Salvadoran farmers can augment corn production over the next few years to a point that national demand is filled without imports. An increasing use of hybrid seed, fertilizers, and mechanical equipment can make this job possible without much addition to the work force engaged in the crop. Increased productivity per acre may also permit the diversion of some favored land to export crops, and some steeply sloping land to orchards.

Corn farmers have never had a strong institution of their own like the centralized producer organizations which serve the three main export crops. Recent productive gains have tended to come under government auspices. Since this is the major crop of the country's small landholders, they are particularly sensitive to the nature of government agricultural programs. Until a producer organization can offer its members services of the magnitude of those enjoyed by export crop producers, the interested government agencies will have to operate in an area of considerable political delicacy. In view of the political demands for more even distribution of land ownership, the government may need to discourage shifts toward large, plantation-type corn growing in the country.

Other Food Crops

The country's second major food crop is grain sorghum, which is used as a low-cost corn substitute. Its cultivation closely follows that of corn growing. At the time corn ears are doubled over for drying at the close of the rainy season, sorghum is planted between the corn rows for maturity at the end of the year. Cultivation methods follow the same techniques which the farmer uses for his corn. At present it is estimated that about 90 percent of the sorghum is used as human food, with the rest employed as animal feed.

Grain sorghum production is a relatively recent introduction to the Salvadoran farm economy compared with corn, but suffers from similar low productivity under present methods. World hybrid sorghum technology, while now about twenty-five years behind similar advances in corn, is developing fast and encourages the hope of much higher yields in the future. As the national supply of cattle and poultry increases and human diets improve, an increasing amount of sorghum production can be diverted to animal feeds.

Beans and rice form important supplements to the basic corn/sorghum component in the Salvadoran diet. Beans are grown throughout the country, usually in association with corn.

The technology employed is usually of the same level that the farmer uses for corn. Under the most primitive conditions, beanstalks twine on the growing corn, partially checking its growth but also checking weeds. At harvest time, when the corn ears are doubled over, bean pods are collected from the field. The farmer puts them in a pile on the ground, and his family threshes them with wooden flails. More mechanized operations use motor-driven threshers.

Rice is grown in limited locations, mostly near the Pacific Coast where the possibilities of irrigation exist. Most of the country's production comes from large plantations specializing in this crop. Reported national crop levels are higher than those recorded for beans, but this may be due to the difficulty of recording the bean production of the nation's small farmers. Rice production still involves high risks from bird, insect, and blight damage, which discourage small farmers from planting it even when their land is suitable. In market terms, however, the future of rice is attractive as a dietary alternate to corn. Human history has shown a tendency to shift diets from corn to rice and eventually to wheat grains as incomes rise. Postwar dietary trends in the Central American country of Costa Rica have illustrated this factor once again. As incomes rise in El Salvador this tendency will probably be reflected there as well, encouraging either increased national rice production, imports, or both.

The country's climate and soil permit the production of a wide variety of other foodstuffs, from tree crops like coconuts through the range of tropical fruits to row crops like onions and radishes. Few growers devote their sole energies to any one of these lesser crops. One reason is the marketing risk always inherent in undiversified production. Another is the ever-present tropical risk of insect and blight damage on concentrated stands of any one crop. As indicated previously, the growing urban population seeks more varied foodstuffs as incomes rise, and profit potentials clearly exist in many fruits and vegetables.

Present truck-garden type production is carried out mostly by small landholders. One large landholder seeking to diversify some of his crop land made a study of the national consumption of radishes. He found that by using available methods on only a portion of his land, he could produce radishes at a lower cost than the national norm, and in effect supply the entire country with cheaper and better radishes than are now being consumed.   He decided against this type of production, however, feeling that it would deprive a large number of small holders of their present supplemental income from the crop.

Though figures for most garden crops are not complete, it appears that a similar situation exists in many of them. If the citizens continue to encourage the status of small landholders, it may be advantageous to avoid unduly large operations in these crops, even though larger farms might achieve economies through their more intensive levels of production.

Miscellaneous Crops

Several field crops are receiving increasing attention in the country, though not for their value as human food. National production of henequen finds its destination in sacking and other fibre usage. Tobacco is grown for cigarette production.

Henequen production is concentrated in comparatively arid areas east of the Lempa River.   The sharp-leaved plant, which resembles a cactus, is planted as a row crop on sloping terrain which has lost most of its value as corn land. Several times a year a few leaves are cut from each plant, with the plant itself remaining in production for many years. Small holders frequently process their own leaves into fiber, which means beating the leaf pulp from its fibrous binder, washing the fibers, and then drying the hanks of fiber in the sun. Larger producers have mechanized these operations to a considerable extent. Laws were passed in the past several decades encouraging increased production; particularly important in this connection is one which requires the export of Salvadoran coffee in locally produced henequen bags. While this permits the industry to thrive within the limits of local demand, it is unlikely that it could compete in international trade with Asian jute.

Tobacco production is carried out on an efficient basis by small growers, under the conditions quite different from other field crops. One large private firm produces most of the country's cigarettes, and it acts as banker, buyer, and farm extension agent for the tobacco planters. The cigarette firm has not endorsed large-scale plantation-type production of tobacco, feeling that encouraging smaller farmers was in its own and the national interest. Farmers are trained in the techniques needed for tobacco production, given crop loans, and encouraged to borrow field equipment from the company to assist them in mechanizing their operations. Tobacco quality standards have been raised to the point that for some stronger cigarette blends, cheap foreign tobaccos must be imported as a supplement. National per-capita cigarette consumption is fairly low, and it appears likely that tobacco will continue to maintain its relatively steady though slow growth curve in the years ahead.

Summary

The domestically consumed crops without export orientation all display common differences from the coffee, cotton, and sugar technologies discussed previously. For the most part, these crops are not grown under plantation conditions, nor does this technique appear necessary. For much of the agricultural population, these are the really vital crops, though public attention usually focuses on the more glamorous export sector alone.

Productive efficiency in the domestically consumed crops is usually low. Technological progress of striking magnitude is clearly possible in corn, and appears likely in other important sectors like beans, sorghum, and fruit cultivation. The insularity of the national market has shielded these crops from international productivity standards. Upward productivity shifts should be encouraged in the non-export crops as well, however, since the gains will necessarily add to national consumption levels.

Unlike the three export crops, the domestic crops as a rule lack producer-controlled self-help organizations. Corn growers, while not yet highly organized, are showing increasing interest in an organization patterned along the lines of those developed in the export fields. The tobacco growers, due to their special relations with the cigarette factory, have some of these advantages already. The remaining crops, however, lack their own special forums. The Ministry of Agriculture and farm technicians from the Agency for International Development work with farmers on these crops, but

governmental suggestions often lack the authority with which
farmers endow their own producers' organizations.

Table 3 below, is constructed along the lines of Table 2,
which showed yield gains in the three export crops. In this
new table, the export crops are aggregated to show their
combined production gains within the last decade. It will be
noted that the four largest domestic crops (corn, sorghum,
beans, and rice) have shown few productivity gains over the
same period. At the same time, the bumper corn and sorghum
crops of 1960/61 give a partial indication of the magnitude
of gains possible in the production of the country's small
farmers.

TABLE 3

Domestic Crop Production and Yields*

Crop	Annual Average 1951-5		Annual Average 1956-60		1960/1 Yield 1951-5=100
	Area	Production	Area	Production	
Corn	17.8	36	17.6	32	110
Sorghum	n.a.	23.9	n.a.	24.3	147
Beans	2.7	4.4	2.3	3.3	75
Rice	1.3	3.6	1.2	3.3	93
All Export Crops	15.0	24	17.8	36	125

*Area in 10,000 hectares; production in 100,000 quintales.

SOURCE: Banco Central de Reserva, Revista Mensual.
Recently revised figures (1963) increase old production estimates for corn, beans, and rice. The new series was used
for sorghum.

CHAPTER 4 ANIMAL PRODUCTION

The striking gain in total production of field crops during the past three decades has not been matched in the development of animal production for human consumption. The average Salvadoran diet is low in its intake of animal proteins, and this deficiency frequently leads to ill health and occasionally to premature death. A large variety of obstacles has impeded animal production, but these can probably be overcome in the decades ahead. The discussion which follows divides animal production into three sectors: cattle and pigs, poultry, and fish.

CATTLE AND PIGS

Traditional Spanish colonial customs still hinder cattle and pig production in El Salvador, as in many other Latin American countries. The early Spanish settlers introduced domesticated cattle and swine soon after their arrival. Isolated plantation owners produced meat, milk, lard, tallow, and hides for their own use on the farm. The early Spanish city founders encouraged farmers to bring these products to the city markets, but soon found that spoilage under tropical conditions made meat and other animal by-products extremely dangerous to use. In self-defense, leaders in urban communities established regulations requiring that animals be delivered alive for slaughtering in controlled locations.

Today the country's larger towns and cities still maintain municipally controlled slaughterhouses, and it is illegal to transport freshly killed meat from one town to another. Butchers at the local slaughterhouses have a traditional craft security which has lasted for centuries, and oppose change in the

present system of local monopolies.   In some cases, the
municipality itself receives considerable income from a tax
on each animal killed.   Under these conditions, freshly
killed meat is the only consumer product which cannot
be freely bought, sold, and transported throughout the
country.

Cattle raising follows a number of patterns in the country.
On the smallest farms, the chief value of livestock is as a
source of motive power.   Oxen, and occasionally cows, are
widely used as draft animals, plowing fields, and moving crops
and farm wagons.   Draft horses are less often encountered,
due to their lower endurance.   Draft animals are kept until
they die of natural causes, and then processed for food on
the farm.

Larger-scale farmers may have a few head of cattle
grazing on land which is not suitable for field crops. Breeding
is usually not controlled, and cows are not milked on a commercial scale.   Cows or bulls are sold on the hoof in nearby
towns for meat when the farmer feels he will obtain an advantageous price or when he needs money -- but the average
age of slaughter is high and the carcass weight low.

A few large farms have diversified into commercialized
cattle raising.   Breeding may be closely controlled, with
calves segregated for meat or milk production.   Steers are
grazed in open fields, provided salt, water, and supplementary feeds under controlled conditions.   Milk cattle receive
careful handlings too, and are milked in milk sheds.   In this
type of operation, the farmer attempts to market his steers at
optimum weight, and he usually has a long-term contract for
milk deliveries.

Pig production generally follows the most primitive
techniques used for unsegregated cattle.   Commercialized
pork production is rare, while the sight of mature foraging
pigs weighing no more than fifty pounds is common. Sheep
are seldom encountered, while goats are somewhat more
common.   These animals, like cattle, must be driven or trucked
live to urban markets.

Under these circumstances, meat quality is low. Slaughter-
house techniques are antiquated, leading to further productive
losses.   National demand for meat sufficiently surpasses local

production to encourage large cattle drives from other Central American countries, as well as the importation of preserved and frozen meat by sea and air. Milk production levels are also haphazard, encouraging a widespread use of imported powdered milk, butter, and cheese.

The Ministry of Agriculture, the Agency for International Development, and a Cattleman's Association have all tried with limited success to improve production in meat, dairy, and animal by-products. It appears essential to replace the archaic slaughtering restrictions with rules which will safeguard public health, yet encourage efficient marketing of meat. The largest cattle raising areas are somewhat distant from the capital, suggesting that the development of regional slaughterhouses near the range would be most efficient. Such a pattern would tend to offset the otherwise unchecked concentration of almost all industrial development in the immediate area of San Salvador.

When cotton became an important export crop, some of the country's best grazing land was diverted to field use. Bearing in mind the limited availability of suitable land not in crops, major increments in cattle and pig production are probably not possible without closer attention to supplemental feeding practices. In addition to natural forage, supplemental food sources are available from corn stalks, grain sorghum, sugar wastes, and oil seed cake from cotton gins. The recent installation of two large wheat flour mills is also providing a new supply of wheat wastes to the country.

POULTRY

The poultry industry in El Salvador is almost entirely in the hands of small farmers. National statistics on poultry and egg production are lacking. Though the raising of poultry for meat does not encounter the legal obstacles raised in the cattle trade, low levels of technology coupled with inefficient marketing practices have kept national poultry consumption at a low level.

Small farmers often maintain a few chickens at their farm site, that live in an almost wild state. Small farms are unfenced, and the birds usually roost in the farmhouse as protection from dogs and other predators. Since roosters are not segregated from hens, the production of unfertilized eggs is sporadic. The birds live on scraps from family meals and on natural forage. Birds or eggs may be consumed at home, or traded with neighbors or in the nearest town.

Somewhat larger operations with a dozen or more birds may involve a bit of supplementary feeding, usually on corn or grain sorghum. Only in a few instances have farmers shown enough interest in commercial poultry production to use commercial food concentrates.

Chickens and turkeys to be sold for home consumption arrive at the market live, and usually are purchased this way. The urban buyer takes the birds home, where they are maintained until they are killed immediately prior to being cooked. Commercial killing and preparation of birds, including freezing, is thus far very limited. Most eggs are marketed in a similar unorganized fashion, though some egg producers near the larger cities have developed relations with bulk buyers in the larger retail outlets.

Within the last decade the Ministry of Agriculture and the International Cooperation Administration have engaged in efforts to encourage increased bird and egg production, though thus far with limited success. Technological knowledge is available for upgrading the blood lines of the country's flocks, and increasing amounts of supplemental feeds are being developed from waste products coming from the country's new wheat flour mills. Latent demand for more poultry and eggs clearly exists, as evidenced by the country's imports of these foods in fresh and preserved forms.

As urban entrepreneurs enter the growing field of food wholesaling, they in turn will probably encourage further national production and improved marketing practices. Over the longer term, there appears to be no reason why the country should not become self-sufficient in poultry and eggs at much higher levels of per-capita consumption. Further improvements in this field appear likely to add another source of cash income to smaller subsistence farmers.

FISHERIES

Though the country has an extensive Pacific shoreline, ocean fisheries have lagged far behind modern capabilities. Until recently, the great majority of the population avoided the low coastal region due to dangers from disease. Residents of the capital (San Salvador is only twenty-odd miles from the sea) distrusted sea food, because it was unfamiliar and because of the risk of poisoning from spoiled fish. The few full-time ocean fishermen attempted to overcome urban suspicion by drying fish at seaside, or bringing live varieties, such as lobster, to city markets. Neither effort met with much success. Fish as such were welcomed as a dietary supplement, however, with imported canned sardines a national favorite.

At present a national ocean fisheries industry is developing around a nucleus of firms catching shrimp for export. Export shrimping began for the first time in 1957, and has since grown to the point that shrimp provide the country's third largest source of foreign exchange after coffee and cotton. At first old boats with foreign crews were employed, but by 1958 the burgeoning industry attracted so much attention that new boats were being commissioned in the United States, and local people were being trained as fishermen, mechanics, and captains. By 1961 the national fleet had increased to 72 boats, while 1960 exports (almost all to the United States) were about 8.8 million pounds.

Shrimp fishing involves netting the bottom-feeding crustacea in relatively shallow coastal waters. When the large nets are brought up, they usually contain a large quantity of sea fish as well. Since these have much less value per pound than shrimp and a limited export demand, they are usually tossed back into the sea. This almost accidental catch of sea fish represents a valuable resource which in time can be developed as a major source of animal protein for the national diet. Experiments are now going on to process the "waste fish," either for direct market sale or as a raw material for fish flour, fish meal, and other fish concentrates.

In contrast to the present national apathy toward sea fish, limited supplies of river and lake varieties find a ready market. Records on catches are not kept by any centralized authority, and most fishing is done by individuals or small family groups.   One fishermen's cooperative controls most of the production at Lake Güija on the Guatemalan frontier. Lake Coatepeque produces fresh-water crabs as well as fish, while Lake Ilopango near the capital has the least fish resources of the country's major lakes.   The Lempa River is extensively fished, as are some of the country's smaller rivers.   Thus far, fish breeding and stocking is rudimentary, though a project with assistance from the U.N.'s Food and Agricultural Organization (FAO) is showing the profits which can come from stocking streams and also from intensive fish farming.

SUMMARY

While the country's meat producing industries have been neglected in the past, it is apparent that sharp growth is possible in animal husbandry, poultry raising, and fisheries. Within the short span of five years, an infant shrimp industry became the country's third largest source of export earnings, indicating the magnitude of possible improvement. Given the present low per-capita intake of animal protein, with its necessarily debilitating effects on health, further growth in meat raising in its various forms can bring both economic and social dividends.

The shrimp fishing industry includes large capital investments in boats and processing facilities, but other meat raising activities are thus far characterized by small scale production and small investments per producing unit. Future trends would appear to be toward more intensive meat raising, instead of further use of practices more appropriate to sparsely settled areas. Intensive methods (in contrast to those used on large ranches) are most suitable for small farmers.

Local demand for meat products is considerably higher than national output, as shown by the high import component in the various consumption categories. This clearly signals economic opportunity for the nation's farmers and fishermen. Rational production goals can seek not only to displace imports, but also to augment production to accommodate an increasing population and higher per-capita consumption levels.

CHAPTER

5 INDUSTRY

The industrial revolution in El Salvador has followed to a considerable extent the process which has taken place in other countries. Before industrialization as such begins, there are usually a cluster of small household production units which process local raw materials for home use and sale in nearby markets. This handicraft stage is present even in more-or-less primitive tribes, but is distinguished by the lack of division of labor, and the lack of mechanical assistance to the workers.

Industrialization itself involves a division of labor among the workers and mechanical multiplication of human force. The industries themselves can usually be separated into two categories which have different national impact: those which process local raw materials, and those which rely on imported raw materials as a basis for their production. At higher stages of development, either category may include some plants which not only conduct operations along lines familiar in other countries, but which have become so advanced and technologically competent that they create new inventions and technological breakthroughs.

Almost all Salvadoran industrialization has taken place in the past three decades. Within this short time span many of the country's most developed raw materials, usually agricultural in nature, have become the basis for local industrial plants. In the past fifteen years industry relying upon imported raw materials has multiplied as well. Technological innovation has also become apparent in the postwar period, distinguishing the country from its neighbors. The following review of Salvadoran industry groups enterprises according to the source of their main raw materials. Despite this division, it must be borne in mind that all Salvadoran industries are, to some extent at least, dependent upon imported fuels, machinery, or other items to operate.

INDUSTRIES USING LOCAL RAW MATERIALS

Textiles

The textile industry is the largest single industrial user of Salvadoran raw materials and labor. Some small plants were already functioning three decades ago, but production was at low levels and technological methods were limited in scope. In the decade of the 1930's some additions to physical plant were made, but the expansion effort was checked by the difficulty of obtaining machinery during World War II. In the immediate postwar period, retooling had to rely on secondhand machinery, which therefore was not of the most modern design.

In the late 1950's a major mill was constructed with Salvadoran and Japanese capital, employing modern machinery and permitting high labor performance standards. This mill is now the largest single consumer of cotton in the country, and although exact figures are not available, it probably has the highest production value of any mill.

The older mills followed an evolutionary process of development, getting many of their original workers from handicraft weaving industries. Work norms froze at a low level in the 1930's, and only with great effort has management been able to retrain workers to higher levels of productivity. At present it is believed that many of the older firms, though admittedly using older machinery, are not yet benefiting from the levels of labor productivity which their machines would permit. With production costs too high, sales are limited and this in turn restricts employment opportunities and wages in this segment of the industry.

The new Salvadoran-Japanese mill started with a different recruitment policy. Management had the alternative of completely training inexperienced employees who had never worked in industry, or of retraining textile employees hired away from the less efficient mills. The firm decided to start with untrained workers and carry the full load of worker education. Within a few months, worker productivity was considerably higher than in the older plants, even in jobs using almost identical machinery.

The results of this approach demonstrate several important features of industrial labor relations in El Salvador. The nation's labor force can be trained to achieve technical skills within a relatively short period of time, provided the proper training methods are used and the workers are properly motivated. Formal education is not a prerequisite for this process, since many of the mill hands are illiterate. A positive approach to employee motivation in this mill has also encouraged workers to increase individual productivity even when automatic pay differentials are not forthcoming. The employee's pride in achieving a new industrial skill is, in itself, a reward which brings social as well as economic benefits.

Facing this new competition, older mills sought to improve plant productivity through increased training, enlarged work norms, and changes in mechanical procedures. The training approach has brought some good results, but enlarged work norms by themselves have been resented by the workers as a "speed-up" technique. Least fruitful were the efforts of several plants to make mechanical changes which would lead to layoffs of some technologically displaced individuals. Plant unions and even the national government have such a large stake in maintaining industrial employment levels that management was dissuaded from proposed equipment purchases. This reaction is likely to persist for some years, in some instances impeding otherwise valuable technological changes.

Further development of the cotton textile industry is clearly possible in the country. With good quality raw cotton available, the main limiting factors at present are high sales prices due to low productivity, and limited variety in the national output. Production runs presumably can increase as the population grows and per capita incomes rise. The addition of variety to production presents more complicated problems. No mill at present makes color-fast prints of the multicolored variety available on an imported basis. The principal reason for this is that the dies for multicolor printing are very expensive, and their cost cannot be justified in production runs of less than several million yards. At the country's present size, it would be quite difficult to sell any one pattern in volume of half a million yards, far below the needed production magnitudes. It may be possible to overcome the limits imposed by die costs if private firms in a number of countries trade dies back and forth after making small runs, amortizing full die costs over a number of marginal runs in several countries.

In 1960 the imported value of cotton threads, semi-finished, and finished textiles was almost as large as the total factory output of the various textile mills. Clearly the local industry will never be able to duplicate the full variety of world textile production, but improvements in costs and styles should have a tendency to limit imports. Major export markets, on the other hand, appear to be out of the question for the near future. Neighboring countries are in roughly the same stage of textile development, while more indus- trialized countries have highly competitive industries already battling for world export markets.

Processed Coffee

Industrial treatment of coffee takes place to some extent in the country's beneficios (see Chapter 3). The Alvarez beneficio in Santa Ana is one of the largest and most highly mechanized in the world. Technical innovations employed there include machine-handling of drying beans, gravity and compressed air separation techniques to remove wastes, and considerable automation as the coffee beans move through the process to the final sorting and bagging as quality-graded coffees. Even at this beneficio, however, the process is extremely labor-intensive. Management's search for labor- saving devices here, as in other beneficios, has been tem- pered by the realization that coffee beneficios are one of the largest sources of employment in the country. In this context, social pressures may be such that technological change will come slowly in this phase of coffee production, leaving it at a semi-industrialized stage.

The country has a number of small roasting mills which process coffee for local consumption. Various grades are bought and mixed, and frequently cereals such as sorghum are added to lower the cost of the final product. At present world price levels coffee is a semi-luxury drink in the country, and national per-capita consumption is estimated to be only half that in the United States. Population increases and improvement of living levels will probably increase the output of the coffee roasters, but may not generate much addi- tional employment demand.

An unusual example of technological skill is provided by the country's first soluble coffee plant, established with local and American capital in the late 1950's. Employing closely guarded trade secrets, the plant processes local beans into soluble powder which is shipped by air to principal American markets. The plant is located close to the Ilopango airport to facilitate these exports. Several varieties of the soluble product are packaged for local sale as well. In addition to soluble coffee, the plant later began large-scale production of other soluble foods, chiefly corn and beans. Due to the extremely high investment in capital equipment, productivity in this plant is probably the highest per man-hour of any industry in the country. Despite its high initial costs, the plant is reputed to be a very successful financial venture, as well as an encouraging example to other investors with industrial ambitions.

Cement and Building Materials

Soon after World War II, interest was revived in the establishment of a cement plant to fill national needs. Until a plant was built at the Pacific port of Acajutla, national demand was met through imports and some local production of kiln-dried lime. This latter product was made by small producers at the country's scattered limestone outcrops, and was of extremely uneven quality. Imports were vital because the country's long record of earthquakes requires shock-resistant cement construction for all larger buildings.

Faced with this opportunity, a number of investors built a plant designed to process sea shells as a source of lime. National demand has continued to increase beyond the plant's present capacity of 2 million bags per year. Years of operation have reduced the supply of shells, and the company is developing alternate sources of supply which include a limestone deposit north of Lake Güija. The pressure of increasing demand is also encouraging study of a second mill, probably at the inland limestone site.

Following establishment of the cement mill, a large number of secondary cement industries also came into existence. These include plants producing cement pipe and tile, cement blocks, and other products for the construction trade. One firm is now producing pre-stressed concrete utility poles, to replace high-cost metal or short-lived wooden posts on the country's power, telephone and telegraph lines. Employment in these secondary industries is considerably larger than at the cement mill which made these plants possible. This multiplying effect, which exists in other industries as well, helps explain the rapidly increasing pace of industrialization in the past few years.

Paralleling the secondary cement industries are firms which make other construction products such as bricks, tile, and piping. In the 1930's, bricks were fired at small kilns with little quality control, but today production is far more advanced. Rapid urban population growth, particularly in San Salvador, presents these industries with excellent prospects. Export opportunities will be limited for most of these products, due both to high transportation costs and competing production in neighboring countries. Even without exports, however, production of cement, its secondary products, and other construction materials should more than double in this decade.

Vegetable Oils and By-products

Expanded cotton production in the postwar period has made possible a major vegetable oil industry. In the 1930's, vegetable oils for cooking and soap were produced in small presses, using limited quantities of cottonseed, coconuts, and tropical olive (aceituno). The main components of the country's present industry use cottonseed as their major source, with other oils added for flavoring and quality characteristics. Vegetable oils have little competition in making products where animal fats might be used were they present in good supply.

While there has been some exportation of industrial grade cottonseed oil to other Central American countries, secondary industries using vegetable oils are expanding production so rapidly that they will soon take the entire national supply. In some cases, oil mills have widened production to include cooking oils and soaps, while others sell most of their production to secondary manufacturers. The largest oil mill also installed a modern new line of margarine-making equipment. Oil cake, which is used as a feed supplement for cattle, is also becoming increasingly important.

The vegetable oil industry is another example (like that of cement and its associated activities) where the multiplying effect of basic industrialization is clearly displayed. In this case the original raw materials (cotton, coconuts, etc.) are gathered in a labor-intensive manner, and then processed in such forms that extensive supplies of capital are needed. The industrial plants are located in San Salvador and other urban centers, rather than near the source of raw materials, to permit rapid distribution of the low-cost consumer end-products. While expansion of this industry has been particularly sharp in the last decade, further growth in per-capita consumption levels appears quite possible. Additional production may also find outlets in neighboring countries. Due to the limited availability of land for cotton raising, the importation of foreign oil seeds may be necessary after further growth in this industry.

Cigarettes

The role of the country's major cigarette plant has been mentioned in Chapter 3 in connection with its development of an advanced tobacco growing system. While this firm is the only one mechanized to the extent that it clearly qualifies as an industry, the bulk of the country's tobacco consumption is presently processed by small household establishments which hand-roll cigars and cigarettes. In the late 1950's the cigarette company moved to a new plant built along the highway between San Salvador and the Ilopango airport. Production ranges through a variety of brands, including filter-tip and mentholated cigarettes. Sales are limited by the high cost of finished cigarettes, caused by a large national excise tax. Export possibilities are slight, since neighboring countries also protect national cigarette production for excise receipts.

With its market possibilities thus restricted, the company's management has proven one of the most resourceful in increasing profits through careful personnel policies. Workers are carefully trained before using the plant's complicated machinery, and a special force of maintenance workers is on hand in case mechanical difficulties should develop. The plant is operated as an independent industrial complex, with such features as a company cafeteria, a medical dispensary, standby electric power generators, water storage and other equipment for fire fighting, and fencing for plant security.

Along with many other industrial plants, the company maintains its own warehouses, delivery vehicles, and machine shop. As one of the country's leaders in employee practices, the firm maintains company athletic teams, and employee fringe benefits beside comparatively high pay scales include working uniforms, paid vacations, sick leave, and retirement pay. Through attention to these details, management has been able to avoid excessive expenses from strikes, high employee turnover, worker negligence, and other costs which plague some industries where personnel planning has been largely ignored.

Beverages

Beverage production is particularly attractive in El Salvador because the semi-tropical climate encourages high consumption throughout the year. The country has one large brewery, and this firm is also a leading producer of soft drinks, ice, and bottled water for home use. Other companies also produce soft drinks, some with international trademarks. A few firms make wines and stronger alcoholic beverages. The production of beer and other alcoholic beverages has not shown much growth in recent years, largely because these products are too highly priced for widespread use. Sales prices before excise taxes are not unusually high by world standards, but distribution is hampered by the low level of consumer incomes and the consequent position of these products as semi-luxuries.

Soft drinks, which sell for about one-third of the cost per ounce of beer, enjoy a much wider market. For these products, children as well as adults are important consumer targets. Sales outlets are not legally restricted, as in the case of alcoholic beverages, and some mechanical dispensers are in place in urban locations.

The country's various beverage industries are important domestic consumers of industrial sugar production. Near the country's new sugar refinery an industrial alcohol plant is being constructed which will increase demand for sugar and its by-products. Expanding needs for sugar will, in time, probably absorb that portion of national sugar production currently exported. It is less likely, however, that beverages themselves will be exported, due to the low value per unit weight and high transportation costs, and the existence of competing industries in neighboring countries.

One recent development in the beverage industry has been an effort to expand secondary production in the field and thereby reduce costs. Bottle labels are locally printed, and production has begun on bottle caps. Several local firms have joined with others in Central America to consider the joint establishment of a glass bottle plant, to displace present heavy imports of containers. An efficient plant, even if located in another Central American country, should materially reduce beverage costs and thereby enable increased penetration of the consumer market.

Henequen Products

One large establishment formed three decades ago is the major user of the country's henequen production. The company's owners also own an important proportion of the plantations growing henequen. Fiber is spun into twine which is later woven into bags or rough textile material. A law requiring that coffee exports be sent out in henequen bags of national manufacture limits competition from imported sacking. In the last several years, coffee export volume has shown little tendency to rise, limiting expansion hopes in this field. Other agricultural products, however, such as corn, can become important users of locally made bags. Henequen textiles are gradually finding another market in the expanding local furniture industry. The mill has also diversified to some extent by spinning cotton and coarser fibers for bagging. With the plant's present capacity, it is unlikely that local demand will require an additional bag mill in the next few years.

Leather Industry

Within the limitations imposed by low levels of cattle production, tanneries operate near the country's major urban slaughterhouses. Hide values are restricted by damage caused by tropical flies, which can permanently scar cowhides. Many of the country's small tanneries use relatively antiquated preparation techniques. In consequence, many of the country's leather-using industries rely upon imported leathers as well as local production.

Shoemaking of the industrial type takes place in two plants, the larger of which employs modern American machinery and produces a wide variety of styles. These firms experience considerable unorganized competition from several thousand individual shoemakers and cobblers scattered throughout the country. Other leather products such as purses, saddles, luggage, and straps are made by small firms and cobblers.

The two industrial shoe firms, both of which were established after World War II, have encouraging growth prospects not only within the country, but also for regional exports. Cost reductions should be possible as installed capacity becomes more fully employed, further widening present markets. More intensive penetration of the national consumer market, while hurting individual shoemakers in their production of new shoes, should augment their repair income and hence not necessarily create unemployment in this sector.

Dairy Products

Several types of dairy activity have developed in El Salvador, chiefly during the postwar period. Milk processing and marketing is carried out by several dairies in the capital, as well as a new cooperatively owned installation in San Miguel. National per-capita milk consumption is low, partly because of low national production levels. Secondary products such as butter and cheese are produced by a number of small firms, some of which use imported dried milk as a supplement to local purchases.

An ice cream and sherbet industry has shown particularly fast growth in the last decade, with aggressive merchandising methods which include the widespread deployment of small ice cream wagons. Given the nature of the country's climate and the relatively low cost of these consumer products, growth prospects appear quite favorable both in the near future and in the decades ahead. Such growth, combined with a slower increase in per-capita milk consumption, will provide increasing opportunity for the country's farming interests, as well as the industrial processors of milk and its by-products.

Other Industries

The nine important industrial groupings thus far considered all produce industrial products worth more than one
million dollars annually. Of these, the textile industry is the
largest, with an output of about $6 million annually, while the
remaining industries have been discussed in order of production levels. Several industrial categories producing less
also deserve mention, since they have the prospects of joining
the ranks of million-dollar industries in this decade.

The country's single iron foundry (the only one in Central
America) is a noteworthy example of entrepreneural skill.
One family of European immigrants started a firm some years
ago which processed imported iron bars and rods for the
construction trade. Much of their processing equipment was
designed and built by the owners, with the eventual ambition
of integrating their shaping operation with the local production
of iron from scrap. At the end of the 1950's the firm installed
a highly complicated electric oven to produce its own pig
iron. By melting scrap purchased throughout the country,
the firm can produce construction shapes of equal quality
and lower costs than imported materials. Since reinforced
concrete construction is preferred to guard against earth-
quake damage, expansion of the firm's output appears well
assured.

A series of small industries have entered the food processing field as candy manufacturers and food canners. The
candy firms are becoming increasingly important users of
industrial sugar production. Market growth appears likely
since imported candy still provides a sizable proportion of
national consumption. The food canners have begun large-
scale operations within the past few years, largely to supply
local demand. Given the ready availability of tropical products, however, some of the canners may in time be able to
develop premium markets in the United States and Europe
as well.

Woodworking has recently progressed from the artisan
stage to the industrial level in a few firms. The country's
supply of commercial timber is quite limited, and for many
end-uses must be supplemented by imported woods from
Honduras and other Central American countries. Industrial products now include plywood, some veneers, and

mass-production furniture.   This last division of the industry has been particularly encouraged by the endorsement of the Sears, Roebuck branch in the country, which affords locally made furniture a prestige retail market.   Since much of the country's quality furniture has hitherto been imported, furniture making should be an area of continued industrial growth in the decades ahead.

INDUSTRIES USING IMPORTED RAW MATERIALS

Food Processing

A food processing industry depending on imported raw materials has expanded sufficiently during the last decade to approach the size of the cotton textile industry. The prime raw material employed is wheat, which until recently usually came into the country as milled flour.

In 1960 one new mill and an expanded plant of an older firm began milling bulk purchases of imported wheat grain. With the enlarged national capacity, the country's bakeries no longer need import flour by the sack. The mills instead import grain by the shipload for bulk storage at the new port of Acajutla, for later bulk transfer to the mill sites in San Salvador.   The mills also produce bran and other components for cattle and poultry feeds. These shifts in the wheat trade are expected to save considerable outlays in foreign exchange while adding to national employment.   If the mills produce flour and feeds at full capacity, it may be possible to export some in the next few years until national demand overtakes production levels.

The country's largest bakeries are located in the capital. The biggest firm has a new plant, employs quite modern techniques, and produces a wide variety of products. Much of the company's success is due directly to the Salvadoran owner, who learned his skills by working in California bakeries for a number of years.   This advanced experience made it possible for him to select proper machinery, tailor products to the local market, and train his employees to good levels of productivity. Older bakeries are finding his competition a spur to similar innovations on their parts. As per-capita purchasing power increases in the country, the consumption of wheat products will probably increase even faster, due to the historic tendency to shift away from corn and rice diets to wheat. This preference, accompanied by aggressive marketing practices, points to the baking industry as one of the prime growth sectors in the industrial economy.

Other food processing sectors which use sizable imports include the beverage and dairy industries already discussed. Beer production requires sizable importation of malt, while the internationally branded soft drink firms import large amounts of beverage concentrates. The dairy industry still uses imported dried milk as well as flavorings, but milk imports will probably drop as the national dairy herd improves.

Building Materials

A number of separate industries relying largely upon imported raw materials produce building supplies for the country's construction activities. The major firms in this field have been formed within the past few years, and their productive history has been one of sharp growth. Combined annual output probably reaches a total value not much below that of the wheat milling and baking industries described above.

Aluminum

Aluminum technology was introduced to the country in the post-World War II period. The first and still most important aluminum product was the framing for louvered windows used in new construction. Postwar design changes brought demand for large proportions of glass in house and office building walls, and casement-type window construction did not permit the ventilation desired in the local climate. At first extruded aluminum shapes were imported in large quantities, and local assembly firms cut imported glass to size and then sold the shapes and glass sections to construction firms. Several years ago a firm with mixed Salvadoran-American capital established an aluminum extrusion plant in the industrial area between San Salvador and the Ilopango airport. It imports industrial extrusion ingot, and produces a variety of shapes which find their chief market in the construction industry. The ready availability of extrusions has also encouraged the expansion of firms making metal furniture. Aided by its strategic location, the extrusion plant also exports to other Central American markets.

Plastics

A large plastic plant began production a few years ago, using imported plastic powders, resins, and chemicals. End products now include a wide variety of items for the construction trade, including plastic tubing, insulation, siding, and decorative materials. The same firm produces fiberglass products as well. In a different aspect of its operations, the plant makes a range of low-cost consumer products, including kitchen and dining ware, small boats, and toys.

Paints

Two firms produce paint for the national market, using imported pigments and other colorants as their most important raw materials. Paint manufacture was encouraged by the high freight cost of imported paints, since most of the paint's weight lies in its water or oil base. The first firm was established in the mid-1950's, and developed its own brand formulas for interior and exterior use. At the close of the decade another firm was formed to produce an internationally known line of paints on a royalty basis. Together, the two firms are cutting sharply into paint imports, and at the same time their advertising, prompt delivery, and lowered prices are encouraging wider national use of paint products.

Textiles

A number of firms, most of them of recent formation, rely upon imports in the production of textiles and clothing. One mill specializes in weaving synthetic materials such as rayon and nylon, with its textiles sold in turn to clothing factories. The clothing firms, whose production is concentrated in lightweight lines, are usually small industries with about a dozen employees. In addition to locally made cotton and synthetic textiles, imported yarns and yard goods are also used.

As the country's cotton mills and the one weaving synthetic fibers expand, their output should become more varied and sell at lower costs. Both these tendencies should encourage expansion of the country's clothing firms. The present decade should also witness some decline in the country's imports of ready-made clothing from outside the Central American area. On the other hand, increased Central American trade in textiles and clothing should provide both opportunity and competition to the country's clothing industry.

Automotive Products

During the postwar period a number of industrial establishments have developed to service the country's increasing
fleet of automotive vehicles. Before the war, the country's
two railroads had established their own heavy machine shops
for repair and construction of parts to supplement imports.
Automobile, truck, bus, and tractor owners lacked such centralized organization, and hence industrial handling of automotive repairs took longer to develop. At present, the automotive product industry consists of three elements: vehicle
assembly, tire recapping, and battery making.

Vehicle assembly operations are of limited scale, largely
handled by two firms. One, dealing in buses, imports major
components by road from the United States, and then assembles
the buses in San Salvador for sale in the country and elsewhere
in Central America. The other operation is carried on by a
branch of an automobile distributor, and the plant assembles
trucks from components shipped in by sea. Neither instance
involves the manufacture of major components nor detailed
sub-assemblies, but these further steps may take place in the
future.

Several tire recapping firms gained market acceptance
after the Korean War. They import camel back and rubber,
and within the industry a range of tires from automobile
lines up through tractor sizes can be recapped. Tire life is
relatively short in the tropics, particularly for those vehicles
employed off the country's main highways. Thus, recaps
afford important savings to vehicle owners and are finding
an expanding market as the country's automotive fleet expands.

Several small firms engage in battery rebuilding, and
one assembles new batteries from imported components.
Tropical conditions tend to shorten battery life, so this industry too provides attractive services to automotive owners.

So far the only full-scale automotive manufacturing plant
in Central America is a tire factory in nearby Guatemala.
Construction of additional plants in El Salvador or other
Central American countries to produce automotive products
will probably require access to the markets of the entire
area in order to produce at optimum levels. Effective demand
for new cars is probably not enough in the entire region to

justify an automobile factory at this time, but additional assembly plants may be feasible. Due to its central location in the regional marketing area, El Salvador will probably be one of the logical sites for any additional plants producing automotive products.

Other Industries

Several other industrial groups of significant size base their production on imported raw materials at present. The most important ones center on chemicals, drugs, and paper products. The country lacks most of the natural building blocks for a basic chemical industry, save for limited production of marine salt. However, several small firms produce industrial gases which are employed by welders and in the soft drink and beer industry. Small amounts of sulphuric acid are also made locally, but not on a full industrial scale.

Drug production is likewise at its infant stages, with present concentration on those products where mixing, diluting, and packaging represent a large proportion of final costs. The largest production runs thus include such lines as patent medicines, aspirin or sodium bicarbonate-based pills, and sterile injection fluids. These are major components of the national demand for medications, and hence the industry has had the opportunity to develop rapidly. Future prospects are bright, not only for expanded sales in the national market, but also for exports to neighboring countries.

The country lacks commercial stands of pulp wood sufficient to support an integrated paper industry. However, paper product consumption is high and expanding, not only in newsprint and white paper lines, but also in packaging materials. Present production concentrates in the packaging field, and includes one new plant producing corrugated cardboard boxes on a large scale, using imported components. Other firms produce light cardboard boxes, which can be locally imprinted for use as containers by retail firms. Another plant recently began large-scale production of paper bags, some of which are also imprinted with the names of retail outlets. Within the limitations imposed by the lack of pulp resources, the paper product industry has shown considerable growth in the past ten years and seems likely to continue expanding.

THE INDUSTRIAL OUTLOOK

Taking Salvadoran industry as a whole, certain salient features stand out. The industrial revolution has come to the country within the memory of the currently active population. Due to its comparative novelty, the process has not had time to develop many of the restrictive aspects which have evolved in some countries with over a century's experience with industrialization. Most of the country's firms have encountered only limited competition within the national borders, but relatively low tariffs have usually averted the danger of monopolistic or cartel-type elevation of prices to artificially high levels.

Labor-management relations have been unusual in that much of the impetus for labor unions has come from alert plant management, which after World War II, encouraged the formation of unions in many firms. Two loose labor confederations exist in the country, but even without their aid, plant unions appear able to develop independent bargaining positions when negotiating plant contracts.

Before the industrialization process began to accelerate in the postwar period, most citizens deplored high import tariffs. Duties furnished the principal source of government revenue, and due to their ease of collection, successive governments have been loath to adopt free trade policies. In the past few years some of the country's industrialists have adopted protectionist goals, providing new allies to those in the government who seek high customs receipts as a continuing source of revenue. These same officials are aware, however, that a high tariff, even if protecting a local industry, dries up imports in the affected line and hence customs receipts. As a result, in some instances the government has proven less anxious than industrialists to provide increased protective tariffs.

In contrast to the normal rise in protectionist sentiment which has usually accompanied industrialization in most countries, important industrial sectors argue strongly for free trade in many situations. The great majority of the country's industrialists have supported a series of laws granting duty-free importation of machinery and raw materials for newly established industries, with these exemptions running for a number of years. A large number of firms are also squarely behind measures to widen trading opportunities with other Central American countries through a free trade area. Management in these cases believes that Salvadoran efficiency will result in a net exportation of industrial products, with area-wide accounts balanced by the importation of other Central American raw materials.

In this connection, the evaluation of Salvadoran industrial development made by observers in neighboring Central American nations provides an instructive measurement of the country's progress. Many Central American industrialists, businessmen, and government officials frankly fear Salvadoran competition should area-wide free trade prevail. A common characterization has been that El Salvador is the ''Japan'' of Central America. An explicit point is usually made that Salvadoran labor costs are lower than those elsewhere in the area, and this is probably true in the sense that labor costs per unit produced are probably lower than in neighboring countries. Thus far, however, there have been no convincing studies showing that industrial hourly wages (including fringe benefits) in El Salvador are lower than in corresponding firms nearby. Rather, the productivity differential made possible by larger-scale production, better management, and an industrious work force represents the real source of competitive challenge in a free-trading situation.

The rapid growth of Salvadoran industrialization has made close statistical measurement virtually impossible. National statistical series covering production are of limited use, since the choice of a base year and firms to comprise the list of surveyed industries naturally omits firms more recently formed. A 1951 Census of Industry listed 502 firms which used motors and employed six or more people. Total industrial employment under this definition was 23,000 people. In 1956 another industrial census was made, using different definitions and counting all firms with five or more employees. By the 1956 count, there were 11,421 ''industrial'' firms employing 63,000 people. The 1956 survey enumerated many activities normally classified as agricultural, such as the coffee beneficios. Despite the lack of comparability with the 1951 census, growth of considerable magnitude had clearly taken place in the five-year span.

Another indication of industrial growth has been the sharp expansion of the corporate form of enterprise in the last decade. In 1951 there were less than 50 corporations operating in the country, and of these most were in commerce or service trades rather than in manufacturing operations. By 1959 close to 300 corporations were in existence, and much of the increase was due to the formation of new industrial firms. While most of the country's industries are owned by a family or small group, a few industrial corporations have been formed by public stock subscriptions and their shares can be transferred without undue limitation.

In 1959 the Salvadoran Industrialists' Association (ASI) was formed, indicating that industrial psychology had developed to such an extent that manufacturers wished to have their own forum. Formerly they had been members of the National Chamber of Commerce and Industry, where most of their associates were principally interested in commerce and the service trades. ASI members still belong to the National Chamber, but the roughly 200 firms connected with ASI recognize that they have specialized interests as well.

The growth of unionization can also be used as an indication of the speed of industrialization. In 1956 there were about 13,800 union members in the country, with the largest single concentration in the country's two railroads. In 1960 there were about 3,000 workers in the railroad unions and other transportation groups (about the same as 1956), out of a total of 21,000 union members. Between these dates, the number of organized workers outside the transportation field increased by about 7,000. Some of this growth represented established industrial workers unionized for the first time, but much of the gain came in firms which were formed during the period.

Comparing the 1956 union figures with those of the 1956 industrial census, it would appear that about a sixth of those defined as industrial employees were then unionized. Defining ''industry'' more closely to eliminate those primarily involved in agricultural enterprises, which are not unionized, the 1956 union membership may have covered closer to half the country's industrial workers. In 1960 this ratio was probably about the same, indicating that there may have been about 36,000 industrial employees. In contrast, it is doubtful that there were more than 1,000 industrial workers in 1930, or more than 5,000 in 1940. The growth of plant unionization illustrates that workers have had the opportunity to think in industrial terms only within the last two decades.

The industrial expansion which lies ahead in the next few years will probably be more rapid, yet more difficult, than the initial efforts of the last three decades. Many of the more obvious industries requiring limited capital and know-how have already been developed. However, the fact that the country now has an industrial base can make further industrialization a more rapid process.

One indication of the difficulty in further industrialization can be expressed in terms of the capital-output ratio; that is, the amount of investment needed to produce a given level of industrial production per year. As a country industrializes this ratio tends to increase, requiring larger and larger amounts of capital for each addition to output, and usually for each additional industrial job. In the case of El Salvador, the capital-output ratio is still fairly low -- perhaps on the order of three-to-one.

This means that at the present level of industrialization, on average an investment of three dollars in industry will produce one dollar of manufactured value (over raw material costs) per year. Naturally the ratio is higher in capital intensive industries like drugs and chemicals, and lower in such fields as most construction materials. It would appear that generally industrial investments in El Salvador have slower payoffs than would be possible by agricultural investments such as growing hybrid corn, or upgrading meat production. A variety of trade and service investments also appear to produce faster capital returns than those experienced in industry.

A potential industrial investor, therefore, must pass up immediate cash returns for other incentives which he considers more important. Perhaps the greatest attraction of industrial investment at its earlier stages is the allure of technology in a country where innovation is rare. The families owning the country's only electric steel oven and the country's largest bakery are two of many examples of those who are so attuned to the mechanical age and so skillful in their fields that they would feel less personal fulfillment in agricultural or commercial activities. This type of personal drive, which is very individualistic and is a characteristic of all entrepreneurs, is usually accompanied by a strong sense of national pride which seeks to elevate the country's world position by increasing its industrial output. This sense of national industrial pride is a potent force which tends to weld the country's industrialists together as a common progressive force.

The incentives attracting white-collar and production line workers to industrial employment can be more readily measured in terms of immediate economic benefits to them. Salaried industrial employees receive pay scales which permit middle-class consumption levels of food, clothing, housing, and discretional items. These white-collar workers are also the pool from which a second wave of entrepreneurs is being drawn, and most are psychologically oriented to industrial careers.

Workers paid on an hourly or daily scale (<u>obreros</u>) receive wages much higher than agricultural day laborers, and can count on fairly steady employment. There is a sufficient differential in consumption levels to indicate that they should be classed as members of the country's lower middle class, along with comparably paid blue-collar government employees and many employees in commerce and the service trades.   Social prestige attached to industrial employment clearly makes it preferable to almost any employee relationship in rural areas.   In the case of some progressive firms, production-line jobs are considered more rewarding from a psychological point of view than commercial or service jobs with the same pay levels.   Part of this differential appears due to the aura of progress which surrounds the country's industrial activities, and part to the fact that industrial wages and fringe benefits have risen considerably in the past decade.

Summarizing the present situation from the individual point of view, it appears that the country has a pool of entrepreneurs committed to industrial development, and this pool is growing rapidly.   Their efforts will be aided by the clear interest of growing numbers of people, both in cities and in the rural areas, to seek industrial employment at both the white-collar and production-line levels.   Given the favorable inclinations of management, capital, and labor, the strongest limitations on the country's industrial growth will probably be set by the over-all national economic situation.

With a small national population, low income levels, limited natural resources, and a brief history of industrialization, El Salvador's progress in this field will tend to be somewhat circumscribed. Many industries existing in other countries will not be economically feasible, due to the lack of essential raw materials, a lack of a nearby market, or a combination of both factors. Surprisingly, management, labor, or capital shortages appear to be far less limiting.

At present, for example, three highly capital-intensive and technologically complex industries are beginning production in the country: an oil refinery, a synthetic fertilizer plant, and a cooper products mill. The refinery will import crude oil from South America, process it at the new Acajutla port, and market gasoline and other by-products in the country and elsewhere in Central America. The fertilizer plant will import raw materials to the Acajutla area and produce sulphuric acid and fertilizers there for regional use. The copper plant, located in the San Salvador area, will process imported ingots into tubes and copper wire for regional sale. The intensive capital needs for the refinery will be met almost completely by major international oil companies, while the other two operations will be financed by Salvadoran, Central American, and other foreign investors. In each of the three plants, foreign technicians will at first assist local recruits in plant operations. The detailed planning devoted to each of these projects represents a strong vote of confidence by foreign as well as local investors in the Salvadoran economy.

In contrast to these highly capital-intensive plants, many of the logical expansion moves in presently established industries will prove far less costly for increased units of production. Expansion of a going industry can be accomplished by present management, usually assisted by the present workforce with relatively small additions. Thus new jobs are not created as rapidly as investment or production expands. Workers seeking industrial employment for the first time, therefore, will probably find their widest opportunities in newly created industries.

Establishing a new national industry presents the greatest challenge to the entrepreneur. He lacks the example of another national firm in the same field to copy, and also must train his own labor force to fulfill the newly devised function. If his purpose is to displace imports of manufactured goods, he can gauge national demand from import data but cannot be certain how strongly foreign brand names and styles are entrenched in the local market.   If he proposes to make a product hitherto not even imported (fish meal or fish flour, for example), his risks are even greater, since there is no simple way to measure demand. Judging by the vigor of Salvadoran entrepreneurs, however, the next decades should see many new industries established despite these risks.

With many of the nation's most alert minds devoted to industrial development, it is also necessary to recall that successful industrial development cannot feed upon itself alone.   End products must finally meet consumer buying power in the market place, and if purchasing power remains limited, industrial progress will be hamstrung.   For this fundamental reason, the most foresighted industrialists are also assisting in raising agricultural productivity and wages to generate the necessary prerequisites for continued industrial advances.

TRANSPORTATION, COMMUNICATION, AND POWER

El Salvador's development in the past three decades has been distinguished by intensive efforts to improve national transportation, communication, and electric power facilities. Despite its rugged terrain the country today has, for its size, one of the most developed series of infrastructure networks in Latin America. It is difficult to account for the high level of public interest in these fields when one notes the comparative apathy in neighboring countries, but the source of these constructive endeavors may come from the same portions of the Salvadoran make-up which have encouraged such rapid industrialization.

TRANSPORTATION

Roads

Roads and streets carry the bulk of the country's merchandise and personal traffic. While animal-drawn carts are still used in rural areas on country trails, the nation's larger cities and towns are connected by a network of all-weather roads which also provide links to neighboring Guatemala and Honduras.

The Inter-American Highway, built in the 1940's, provides the backbone of the highway system, running from the Guatemalan border on the west through to the Honduran border on the east. Its paved surface links the country's four largest cities (Santa Ana, Santa Tecla, San Salvador, and San Miguel), all of which are in the country's central, mountainous zone. This route carries the bulk of national and international road traffic, and further improvements may be necessary due to this high density.

A second major road, the Littoral Highway, was built along the Pacific coast in the late 1950's, and completed in 1961 with a bridge connection with Guatemala across the Rio Paz. Foreign exchange costs for the Littoral Highway were met by loans from the International Bank for Reconstruction and Development (IBRD). Portions of the road run on cliffs above the Pacific, displaying some of the most spectacular ocean scenery in the Western Hemisphere. The entire route was designed to open up hitherto undeveloped agricultural lands along the coast, and has been quite successful in this endeavor. In addition to providing a link with Guatemala, the road connects the important ports of Acajutla, La Libertad, and La Unión with the farming centers of Zacatecoluca and Usulután.

Other major highways in the country include a route from a second bridge connection with Guatemala, thence running north through Ahuachapán, Santa Ana, and up to the northwest corner of the country near Metapán. Further east, a highway from Acajutla runs northeast through Sonsonate to meet the Inter-American Highway between Santa Ana and San Salvador. A main north-south road through the capital connects the Littoral Highway on the south with the Honduran frontier city of Ocotopeque to the north. Another north-south road runs from the Littoral Highway through San Miguel and San Francisco Gotera to the central section of Honduras.

A maze of secondary and tertiary roads supplement these main arteries. Even at the height of the six-month rainy season, enough are sufficiently maintained so that vehicles can move between most towns with populations of 1,000 or more. In addition to private vehicles and trucks, an extensive system of private bus lines provides low-cost passenger service throughout the country. The high density of road connections is an important factor in making citizens unusually aware of population pressures, since no region is truly isolated from any other.

With the country's main routes already constructed, the government now bears large maintenance expenses which are sure to mount in the years ahead. New construction already planned includes feeder roads connecting with the Littoral Highway. These are mostly farm-to-market routes, and are also receiving assistance from the IBRD. In addition, the government is studying improvements on the Inter-American Highway, which may include a bypass around the increasingly congested center of the capital.

The total number of automotive vehicles is expanding sharply. In addition to wearing out established roads, these vehicles are also forcing additional improvements in city streets. In the years ahead highway and street expenses appear likely to continue requiring their present large proportion of national budgetary expenditures.

The growth in vehicular traffic in recent years is in part indicated by figures on the number of motor vehicles in the country, shown in Table 4.

TABLE 4

Motor Vehicles by Type and Year*

Year	Cars	Buses	Trucks	Total
1947	3,315	567	556	4,438
1951	7,627	1,003	2,364	10,954
1962	19,800	1,450	13,700	34,950

*These figures probably understate vehicles owned by the national government.

SOURCES: Figures for 1947 and 1951 from U.N.: El Transporte en el istmo Centroamericano; 1962 data from U.S. Department of Commerce: Basic Data on the Economy of El Salvador, 1963.

Railroads

Two foreign-built railroads serve the country. Both were constructed in the first two decades of this century. The country's original, locally owned railroad, which ran from the capital west to the coffee center of Armenia, has long since ceased to exist due to highway competition.

The Salvadoran Railways Company, Ltd. (a British concern) until 1962 operated a line connecting the capital, Santa Ana, Sonsonate, and the Pacific port of Acajutla. Virtually all its line is paralleled by heavily used highways, and the company has suffered major losses in both freight and passenger traffic. At the close of 1961 the government granted the line a subsidy to meet payrolls on a temporary basis. The firm's railroad concession was to expire in the early 1970's, at which time the contract provided that the line would be delivered to the government without any liquidating payment.   Due to this provision, company stockholders were understandably reluctant to invest additional funds in the line in recent years.   Operations were completely taken over by the government in 1962.

Prospects appear somewhat less bleak for the other rail line, which is operated by the International Railways of Central America (IRCA).   Track in El Salvador runs from the Pacific port of La Unión through the capital into Guatemala, crossing the border near Metapán.   The Salvadoran division of IRCA has been relatively more profitable in recent years than the Guatemalan division, which connects that country's capital with the Mexican border, the Caribbean coast, and El Salvador. A fair amount of Salvadoran international trade uses IRCA to provide access to El Salvador's Pacific port of La Unión and Guatemala's Puerto Barrios on the Caribbean.   Passenger traffic, on the other hand, is dropping due to highway competition.   Over the longer term, highway competition may be expected to increase for this railroad as well as the other line, and expansion of the country's railway system does not appear likely.

Air Transport

The country moved rapidly into the air age during World War II, when improvements were made on the international airport at Ilopango.   Lying to the east of the capital in an area now almost absorbed by the expanding city, this field provides connections with all Central American capitals as well as more distant locations.   The major passenger carrier using the field is Pan American World Airways, and freight carriers include that line and a number of others which link Central America with Mexico and the United States.   Until recently the airfield was only suitable for the largest propeller craft, but work has now been completed to expand facilities to accommodate jet aircraft.

Given the speed and ease of air transportation, further sharp traffic growth appears likely across the country's frontiers.   The capitals of bordering Honduras and Guatemala are each about an hour away by propeller craft, compared with a day's drive by car.   The growth of passenger and freight business on international routes will probably not be matched by growth in internal air transportation.   Here the country's limited area precludes such development.   The major use of local aircraft at present is for crop dusting -- chiefly in the cotton areas. There is virtually no internal use of aircraft for personal transportation, except by a few plane owners. This pattern of limited use of light aircraft is expected to continue, even if the country's auxiliary airfields improve.

Sea Transport

The great bulk of the country's imports and exports cross the frontier at the country's three Pacific ports of La Unión, La Libertad, and Acajutla. The first is located on a bay at the far east corner of the country, while the other two have open roadsteads but are closer to the capital and other major markets. The Acajutla Port Authority (CEPA), a semi-autonomous organization, has recently completed construction of a new breakwater pier at Acajutla which is employed to handle the largest ships serving the country.

Sea transportation has for years provided adequate means of moving bulk goods to and from the country's distant markets. Coffee, for example, goes almost entirely to the United States and West Germany, while the country's cotton exports are destined for Japan. Bulky imports (industrial raw materials, fuels, etc.) are also best handled by sea from their distant sources of supply. On the other hand, trade with a high value per pound is moving by air to an increasing extent. Passenger traffic was the first to be lost to the airlines. Now the country's exports of soluble coffee and frozen shrimp, as well as imports of luxury goods and many household appliances, move by air as well.

With the growth of air transportation, the gross tonnage of trade through the country's ports is tending to stabilize. Increased trade with other Central American countries, which is a national goal, will probably move for the most part by road and air. Air competition will probably limit gains in other sectors. The country's three ports have a handling capacity considerably above present needs, and with proper maintenance and some modest improvements should serve the country for many years to come.

COMMUNICATION

Mail

The national post office, long a state monopoly, embraces a system of modest size and performance. Mail service within the larger cities is fairly prompt, but inter-urban and rural mail deliveries are often undependable. The lag in postal development is due to the limited financial support received by the post office system, and reliance on alternate forms of communication such as telephone and telegraph. As communications traffic increased rapidly in the past three decades, it outstripped internal facilities to a much greater extent than international mail, which has been given first priority by the post office and moves rapidly.

Telephones

The national telephone system is also a state monopoly. Like the mails, growth in demand has overloaded the telephone system, particularly in the past few years. The total number of telephones in service remained roughly stable from 1940 to 1950, and then tripled in the next decade to a level of about 14,000 lines. At present the government is obtaining financial and technical assistance from the IBRD to bring about a major expansion in the telephone system.

Most telephones are located in the capital and its immediate suburbs. Emergency lines provide at least one phone to several hundred of the country's smaller towns, and the cities have local exchanges tied in to the national network. International land connections to neighboring points in Central America are undependable, but cable and radio telephone service to more distant points in North America and Europe is better. One aspect of the phone expansion presently contemplated would include microwave links in an international network. This is being designed to connect the North American microwave chains with a projected system extending through Mexico and Central America to points in South America. Expansion of this sort appears clearly desirable, and internal telephone development even more pressing -- but these are very expensive steps to take.

With the almost emergency need for improved telephone service, and the high expenses looming ahead, some thought is being given to creating a semi-autonomous utility to manage the country's telephone system. Such a plan could attract private as well as government funds to the capital expansion program, and perhaps include subscriber stock equity as has been successfully developed in Mexico. The government, of course, would continue to regulate rates. Unless the government can enlist aid in some manner, it will have to face capital costs in its telephone system on the same order of magnitude which it is currently spending on road construction and maintenance.

Telegraph

A national telegraph system is operated as a state monopoly, and provides more efficient service than telephones to most of the country's outlying communities. Land links are included to other national systems in neighboring Guatemala and Honduras. Traffic has roughly tripled since 1940, and transmission facilities do not appear to be excessively overloaded when compared with the mail or telephone systems. Even in San Salvador, where mail and telephones are most efficient, considerable use is made of the telegraph system and its messenger service to transmit messages within the city. In addition to the national telegraph network, each of the country's two railroads maintains its own lines for traffic routing and maintenance.

International telegraph service, both by radio and cable, is provided by the national monopoly and several international communications firms. Traffic is impaired by the need to repeat messages over a number of relay points located outside the national territory. International service does not operate around-the-clock unless these foreign relay points are alerted well in advance to remain open for anticipated traffic. Under these limitations, the introduction of teletype operations and other modern communications developments is handicapped. Future increases in the telegraph system, which could include teletypes, telescribers, and other units will probably occur slowly but have less priority than improvement of the telephone system.

Radio

The government operates a number of radio networks in such departments as the Army and the National Police. Its longwave broadcast system includes one major radio station located in the capital, with repeater stations elsewhere. The bulk of long-wave transmission is from privately owned companies, mostly located in the capital. There is limited commercial shortwave broadcasting, but most of this equipment is used by amateur operators. Several firms with extensive operations throughout the country also use shortwave communications sets to coordinate their activities.

The development of high-powered transmitters and cheap receiving sets has produced a communications revolution in the last two decades. For many outlying areas, radio broadcasts of news, music, and other programs form the principal means of contact with the rest of the country and the outside world. In rural areas where illiteracy is particularly high, radio broadcasts have introduced a level of sophistication which would have been impossible under other circumstances. While the total number of radio stations may not increase materially in the next few decades, the impact of the present transmitters will probably continue to expand noticeably.

Television

Two television stations were organized toward the close of the 1950's, both with their main studios in the capital. Reception range covers much of the country, since transmitting locations are atop high terrain. Most television sets at present are installed in the capital and other large cities, and in television homes, viewership has largely displaced radio listening. Programming includes filmed material obtained from the United States and other countries in the hemisphere. Local shows are also produced which have demonstrated considerable technical competence. An effort is now underway to link the country's stations with others in Central America and the United States to provide a pool of programs of common interest. Further sharp growth of the television industry appears inevitable, with its attendant effects on national communications and marketing.

ELECTRIC POWER

In the late nineteenth century, San Salvador was one of the first cities in the world with its own electric power system. Following this early introduction of electricity, however, development lagged because the country lacked fuels for the early generators. The location of main urban areas was too far from good sources of hydroelectric power for feasible small scale development, while imported coal or petroleum products were very expensive fuels for thermal generators. A foreign-owned firm developed its own power and transmission lines to serve the capital and a number of other cities from various generating locations. A number of other small utilities operated on a limited scale at scattered points. By the 1930's most industrial users of power or large enterprises in rural areas relied on their own diesel generators to produce power for business use, while most towns and homes had no power available. The rapid growth of electric power utilization after World War II is discussed below in terms of generation and distribution.

Electric Power Generation

It was not until the postwar period that serious consideration was given to large scale development of the country's hydroelectric potential. Previously such programs had been deterred by their high cost and the distance of generating locations from use centers. A number of technical studies were encouraged when a power shortage became apparent after the war.

Building to some extent on previous tradition, Salvadorans established a semi-autonomous organization known as the Comisión Ejecutiva Hidroelectrica del Rio Lempa (CEL), the bulk of whose board members were private citizens. They were authorized by the government to contract a loan from the IBRD for a large power dam on the Rio Lempa, with a government guarantee standing behind the CEL debt. The government further granted tax-free status and a guarantee to bonds for local sale, which provided the CEL with funds for local currency construction costs. In late 1949 arrangements were completed for the various loans needed to produce the Fifth of November dam on the Lempa River.

In 1954 the first two 15,000 KW generators began transmitting power from the Fifth of November dam. The CEL maintained a high voltage line to the capital, and delivered all its power at wholesale rates to the utility there and other established distributors elsewhere. At the time that this power became available, there were also about 40,000 KW of installed capacity in all the rest of the country put together -- much of it at small private generators as noted above. The sudden jump in generating capacity gave the country its first power surplus in recent years.

Following the introduction of inexpensive hydroelectric power, many smaller generating units were put on standby. Meanwhile, the CEL's directors continued to program additional generating units on the Lempa to keep ahead of national needs. The Fifth of November dam now has two additional 15,000 KW units installed, and a fifth is planned. Work is now going forward to complete a new 15,000 KW unit at the mouth of Lake Güija.   Due to this forward planning, which has been assisted by additional loans from the IBRD, El Salvador continues to be the only country in Central America without a chronic power shortage in its urban areas.

Further hydroelectric power development of the Rio Lempa watershed is already on the CEL's planning boards, and should take care of the country's needs for the next several years. Additional projects are being studied for the Acajutla port area, where a large thermal generating system might be installed alongside the oil refinery.   Further in the future may lie efficient development of the country's geothermal resources from geysers and hot springs in the Ahuachapán area.   These resources, if they could be brought into production, could provide massive increments to national power production.

Power Distribution

Power distribution systems in the country range from the capital's large private utility through smaller units. Some of these are privately owned, some have joint private and municipal ownership, and some are small user systems maintained by industries and agricultural enterprises.   The country's high tension lines are owned and operated by the CEL, and now link all the country's major utilities. When the additional production at the Lake Güija location comes on stream, this will become a true interlocking power net, with the advantage of using alternate production points.   Plans are also going forward to link the CEL system with points in Guatemala and Honduras for international power interchange.

The utility located in the capital, as well as others in the country which distribute power to the general public, operates under national regulations which prescribe minimum standards and control rates. Power rates in San Salvador are among the lowest city rates in this hemisphere. Through careful management, the city's utility has been able to channel its funds into a fairly rapid and continuous expansion, while still maintaining profitable operations. Smaller utilities located elsewhere, while lacking the large management force available in the capital, have also in many instances financed considerable growth by a careful husbanding of resources.

During recent years, the political atmosphere for private utility operation has been good. Unlike the situation in some other countries, the populace and government have shown little interest in diverting public funds to buy out private investors in this field. Salvadorans who have studied the question point out that in other Latin American countries where such policies have been followed, national treasuries disburse large sums to acquire assets which are already installed and functioning. Salvadorans, on the other hand, have preferred to channel government capital investments into creating additions to national wealth, such as roads, schools, and housing.

If this operating framework continues, it appears likely that utility development will continue at its present rapid rate. The farsighted policies of the CEL, which keeps raw power capacity ahead of demand, permits utilities to devote their activities to promoting increased sales to new customers as well as established clients. Aggressive marketing of electricity is particularly welcomed by industrialists, who need not fear that proposed new plants or plant additions will be prevented by a power shortage.

The most difficult problems in power distribution are encountered in the more remote rural areas, where demand per square mile is quite low compared with the situation in the towns and cities. The CEL, together with the government, has made several studies of the possibility of establishing a rural electrification system. This might be done with or without the participation of private capital. Installations of this nature at first are frequently not profit-making, due to the comparatively high line costs needed to reach scattered small consumers. If pursued by a governmental agency or semi-autonomous entity using government credit, such a program might be justified by the growth in productivity and improved social conditions which electrification could bring in rural areas.

In summary, at present there are clear prospects for increasing industrial, commercial, and home use of electric power. Rural electrification of some type probably does not lie too far ahead. In this context, power distribution should continue to be one of the prime growth sectors in the national economy.

7 FINANCE

The financial institutions of El Salvador have undergone such important changes in the past three decades that they have little similarity to their precursors. The sums of money handled in private and government finance have increased greatly, requiring far more sophisticated management techniques. In the early 1930's three separate banks issued legal tender, and in much of the country private currencies (finca money) circulated as well. Legal tender generation was centralized in 1934, and by 1960 coinage and bills in circulation had increased fifteenfold. Government receipts and expenditures increased tenfold in the same period. The following discussion of Salvadoran finance includes the Central Bank, private banking, and government finance.

THE CENTRAL BANK

The Central Reserve Bank of El Salvador was established in 1934, putting an end to a period of banking disorganization which reached its peak during the Depression. Prior to its establishment, three Salvadoran banks enjoyed the right of issuing paper currency, while the national treasury issued silver coinage. The three banks could issue paper money up to twice the value of their subscribed capital, while maintaining a 40 percent reserve against the currency they put in circulation. Under this type of organization, depressed business conditions encouraged the banks to call loans, thereby restricting currency in circulation and producing a spiraling deflation. Government coinage would simultaneously disappear through hoarding, encouraging the emission of finca money, and other forms of private money. This system broke down in the Depression, forcing the government to declare paper and private monies inconvertible into coinage.

In 1933 the Salvadoran government bought out one of the country's three currency-issuing banks, and then sought advice from a British financial expert to convert it into a central bank.   The newly designed institution was unusual in that it was patterned in many ways after the Bank of England. The basic law regulating its functions carefully provided that the national government could not hold stock in the bank, since it was feared that otherwise the credit function would become subject to political manipulation.   Four director positions were established, with these directors to be elected by votes of the bank's shareholders. These directors in turn selected the bank's president, subject to the veto of his name by the national President.

Within this framework, the Central Reserve Bank was given authority to issue currency, act as fiscal agent and depository of the national government, and advance credit to commercial banks and private individuals and firms. It was assigned the power to buy and sell gold, and in the last decade was also empowered to create a market for the securities of the government and the semi-autonomous agencies. The bank was not given the power to supervise private banks, this function remaining within the national government's sphere. In 1961, an amendment to the bank's charter changed the method of electing directors so that the national government gained a direct voice in its operations.

The establishment of a solid circulating currency was the first priority for the newly established bank in 1934. Privately issued bills of hand and finca money were displaced by Central Bank notes, restoring order to the average citizen's financial operations.   In the first ten years of its functioning, little was done in the field of advancing credit to the private banks, since business activity was not expanding and the commercial banks wished to avoid the controls implicit in re-discount operations.   Acting as the government's agent, the Central Bank managed government deposits. It added to the country's store of gold and foreign exchange reserves when increased wartime prices raised coffee receipts without off-setting imports.

The postwar period has seen steady growth in the Central Bank's role in the economy.   In its capacity as government fiscal agent, it has participated in the negotiation of international loans.   Salvadoran memberships in the International Monetary Fund (IMF), the IBRD, the Inter-American Development Bank, and the Central American Development Bank have all been carried out through Central Bank participation.

With the requisite upgrading of its responsibilities, the Bank's staff has acquired specialized training which makes it an attractive labor source to fill ministerial and subministerial posts in the national government.

Booming postwar economic conditions, chiefly due to rising coffee prices, encouraged private banks to use the Central Bank's rediscount facilities for the first time. As the supply of Central Bank credit represented increasing proportions of outstanding bank loans, the Central Bank began to gain a determining voice in national interest rates and credit levels. During the sharp recession which occurred after the 1960 revolution, Central Bank action was a major factor in preserving the stability of the national currency.

The Central Bank staff within the past decade has developed increasing skill in preparing detailed studies of the national economy, including estimates of the gross national product. Together with publications of the Ministry of Economy and the national Census, these reports have created an essential literature regarding economic aspects of the country which is of particular importance to the country's businessmen. As the fund of information regarding the national economy increases, it has also permitted more enlightened action and advice on the part of the Central Bank.

PRIVATE BANKING

Private banking institutions have multiplied in number and importance since the early 1930's, when the country had only four banks. At that time, a majority of the country's citizens probably lived outside of what is normally regarded as a money economy. In rural areas particularly, finance was limited to the activities of local money-lenders, and their operations were little advanced over those employed centuries before. At present, private banking has grown to include commercial banks, mortgage banking, and other institutional lending, with private money-lending on a significant, but far less important scale.

Commercial Banking

Commercial banking in El Salvador three decades ago had only limited development. The four banks then in existence were mainly engaged in financing international trade, and in the case of three banks, issuing currency. Other fields of commercial bank activity such as checking accounts, savings deposits, and loans for real estate, commerce, and industry, were virtually ignored. These neglected fields today comprise the major activities of the redesigned commercial banks.

Following the absorption of one bank to form the new Central Bank in 1934, the other two currency-issuing banks sold their currency and corresponding reserves to the Central Bank. Of these banks, only the Banco Salvadoreño continues to operate today. Once Central Bank operations had assisted in stabilizing the national currency, the atmosphere was cleared for a steady development of banking facilities throughout the country. The first step was the creation of a national mortgage bank (see below) in 1935. In 1937 a branch of the Bank of London and South America (now Bank of London and Montreal) was established. Following World War II, the Banco de Comercio (1950), the Banco Agricola Comercial (1954), the Banco de Credito y Ahorros (1955), the Banco Capitalizadora y de Ahorros (1956), and the Banco de Credito Popular (1958) entered the commercial banking field.

Commercial banks in El Salvador, as elsewhere, limit their credits to short-term loans running up to about a year. In the case of prime borrowers, such as the Cotton Cooperative and the Salvadoran Coffee Company, little difficulty was experienced in refinancing or extending loans as they came due. Major loans of the principal private banks became so highly regarded in the postwar period for their security that American banks advanced these banks funds against their prime credits. In effect, this gave the larger banks access to the American capital market (and hence the United States Federal Reserve System) as an alternative to discounting loans at the Salvadoran Central Bank. Though American funds proved somewhat more expensive than Central Bank money, these lines of credit were used to avoid undue commitment to the Central Bank rediscount system.

In the postwar period, Salvadoran bank rates have been among the lowest in Latin America. Given the nature of the economy, particularly with its strong seasonal demand for credit at the harvest period, it would have been financially possible for the banks to have charged interest rates at least double those in effect, and thus greatly increase net income from operations. Higher rates of this magnitude would have been more in line with those charged in neighboring countries, and probably would not have materially rationed credit or reduced business activity. However, the banking community instead viewed its position as a central one in national economic development, and considered the extension of low but still profitable rates as its contribution to economic expansion.

While the borrowing public did not criticize the lending rate structure, other limitations of the banking system have been felt. Since the country lacks an organized capital market, potential longer-term borrowers felt that the banking system should somehow accommodate their needs. Some steps in this direction have been taken by the creation of several institutions which can keep long-term mortgages in their portfolios, and the establishment of private venture capital funds.

Mortgages and Other Specialized Banks

In 1935, after the national economic system had recovered from the depths of the Depression, a National Mortgage Bank was formed to provide long-term mortgage credit for the first time. The bulk of the bank's capital was provided by the Salvadoran Coffee Association and the Salvadoran Cattlemen's Association, though some was subscribed by private individuals. This bank was empowered to extend mortgages on farm or urban properties. To obtain additional funds, it in turn issues bonds which are absorbed by other banks and also sold to the general public. In late 1961 the total value of these outstanding bonds passed 100,000,000 colones for the first time.

Due to the primarily agricultural interests of the sources of its capital, the mortgage bank's loans have been heavily oriented toward rural properties. More urban-oriented investors formed Crédito y Ahorros, S. A., as an institution to lend money on urban real estate. Instead of issuing bonds, this firm operated somewhat like a savings and loan society, using members' deposits to provide funds for mortgage lending. After the Korean War this institution was converted into a full-scale commercial bank, but it still continues important mortgage activities. A similar history was shared by Capitalizadora de Ahorros, S.A., which today also functions as a commercial bank.

The growth of demand for housing in the postwar period was also matched by the demand for savings institutions in the urban areas. The established commercial banks formed savings divisions complementing their normal commercial operations, and used the savings deposits thus acquired to issue mortgages on their own accounts. Time and savings deposits, virtually nonexistent in 1950, by the early 1960's were roughly equal to all sight deposits in the banking system.

Other Lending Units

The Salvadoran Coffee Company and the Salvadoran Cotton Cooperative conduct financial operations of a magnitude equal to most banks. From their own assets and bank lines of credit, they disburse credit to their respective crop producers, processors, and exporters. Though these organizations do not accept deposits or engage in most of the normal functions of commercial banks, their lending activities are still vital to the economy. In addition to domestic sources of capital, both organizations also acquire funds for their lending operations from American banks and foreign importers.

Insurance firms operating in the country are becoming an increasingly important source of development funds. In addition to normal cash reserves, their portfolios include bonds issued by the semi-autonomous institutions like the CEL and CEPA, bonds of the mortgage bank, and mortgage, commercial, and industrial loans made directly by the insurance firms.

A specialized lending organization known as the Federación de Cajas de Crédito operates throughout the republic, chiefly in small towns. The Federación was set up during World War II to provide loans outside the major cities, at a time when the geographic dispersion of commercial banks was very limited. In the postwar period the commercial banks have created many branch operations, but the Federación still fulfills a useful function and continues to receive government assistance. After the Korean War, the Federación through its semi-independent small lending agencies increased its impact by beginning lending activities among the market women throughout the country.

In a more direct manner, the government began lending operations in the postwar period by establishing the Salvadoran Development Institute (INSAFOP), recently re-named INSAFI. This organization is empowered to lend government funds to enterprises which have strong development possibilities, yet cannot be accommodated by normal banking operations. The institution also has a technical branch which makes detailed studies in the field of national development. Thus far operations have shown moderate success, though the banking community frequently charges that the institute's loans have too often been made in response to political pressures rather than developmental considerations.

Commercial credit operations, such as those between a manufacturer and his suppliers, are an important, though untabulated, part of the Salvadoran financial system. A large volume of farm credit is advanced by coffee beneficios, the cigarette company, and other centralized food processors who have better access to the capital market than the small growers. An extensive system of subsidiary consumer credit is also maintained by retailers, particularly in the larger towns and cities.

Despite the proliferation of organized financial operations throughout the country, private money-lenders still operate to a considerable extent, both in rural and urban areas. While the volume of their activities has probably increased in the postwar period, institutional lending has taken over a much larger share of total national financing. Private money-lending rates are high in El Salvador, but probably lower than in neighboring countries due to competition from financial institutions. In the years ahead as branch banking continues to entrench itself, the individual money-lenders will probably tend to lose ground even further.

GOVERNMENT FINANCE

The tenfold increase in government receipts and expenditures in the past thirty years is one measure of the sharp growth of government finance in the last three decades. A modest amount of the increase is due to inflated prices, but most represents increased government expenditures for health, education, public works, and other socioeconomic activities. The large growth took place without major deficit financing, and the record indicates an over-all national budget surplus for the period as a whole. El Salvador is one of the very few countries in the world which has not increased its internal public debt greatly since before World War II.

Government budgets are prepared by the Treasury Ministry and approved by the National Assembly and President by the start of each calendar year. The detailed national budget includes both capital accounts and salary computations for each government job. Separate subsidy accounts are kept for government aid to city and town budgets, autonomous government institutions such as the Social Security system, and semi-autonomous organizations such as the CEL.

The bulk of government revenues come from taxes and duties on products moving in international trade. Chief among these are coffee and shrimp export taxes, and a wide range of import duties. The next major source of revenue comes from internal excise taxes such as those on beverages and cigarettes. Direct income taxation of corporations and individuals provides the third major source of income. The emphasis in tax legislation has generally been to provide revenue sources which represent small tax-gathering problems. Changes in export prices for coffee showed how vulnerable this approach can be under adverse conditions, for in 1960 the coffee export tax (the prime source of government revenue only a few years before) dropped to the same level as the sum of internal excise taxes on liquor, beer, soft drinks, and cigarettes. With this recent experience in mind, and social ends in view as well, government thinking now appears directed toward increased emphasis on direct taxation, particularly on larger corporate and private incomes.

Government expenditure methods have generally been designed to avert the generation of an overpowering centralized bureaucracy. While the national government has the only important taxing authority in the country, municipal expenditures are met by subsidy grants directly to municipal authorities who establish their own payrolls. Some expenditures are also financed by subsidies to the governors of the country's departments. The Ministries of Education and Defense have the largest ministerial payrolls, while the Ministry of Public Works conducts much of its construction activity by hiring private contractors who in turn supply their own work forces.

FAITH AND CREDIT

In general, Salvadorans have developed an approach to fiscal affairs which is not encountered in many other nations. Two aspects of Salvadoran finance -- low interest rates and the lack of government-sponsored inflation -- are sufficiently different from the practices in most other countries to merit special attention.

As has been noted previously, the Salvadoran population
is relatively small and homogeneous. Few in the society live
far removed from the productive process -- be they engaged
in agriculture, industry, commerce, or other activities. Perhaps their closeness to national activity permits an unusually
large proportion of the population to see a relationship between their work and that of others in different fields.
Such an outlook would appear to lie behind the refusal
of bankers to limit their attention to their own profit-and-
loss statements and charge interest rates as high as the market
could bear. Bank managers and bank stockholders in the country are frequently engaged in other productive activities
as well, either through ownership, management responsibilities, or a combination of both. An industrialist who also is
a bank director may feel that he is only robbing Peter to
pay Paul if he charges high interest rates on industrial
loans in his banking capacity, and then must pay the high rates
as an industrialist. Since bank ownership is concentrated
along somewhat the same lines as industrial production and
export crop production, the compromise between dual interests
is probably a recurring phenomenon in bank management.
Low lending rates as practiced in the country have not
meant disproportionately low rates paid on individual savings.
The spread between payments on time and savings deposits
and the prime lending rate is not nearly so large as that which
has been accepted as normal in many parts of the United
States. The closeness of the rate paid for savings perhaps
reflects in part the alternate opportunities available to the
saver through government-endorsed bonds of the semi-autonomous agencies, and the even higher yields possible through
private money-lending or private investment.
Taking into account both lending and savings rates, the
Salvadoran banking system appears to be well designed to
spur the growth of a national middle class. The availability
of relatively low-cost credit often is essential for the continued development of individual entrepreneurs in the course
of their activities. The creation of a stable, interest-paying
pool for family savings permits lower income families to set
aside funds for purchases of durable goods or capital investments which will in time identify them as members of the
middle class.
Government-sponsored inflation, had it taken place under
these banking conditions, would have cancelled their effects.
A depreciating currency would make banking unprofitable at
low interest rates. Inflation would also operate immediately

to depreciate the savings of the growing middle class and thus sterilize the country's major pool of entrepreneural talent.

Postwar experience with inflation in this hemisphere has given repeated examples of situations in which the middle class has been caught in this classic vise. On the other hand, there is little indication that the richest in a given society have been handicapped much by inflation, since their assets are usually so large and flexible that they can re-adjust easily to changing price levels. For limited periods of time poorer groups have occasionally benefited, particularly if the government used its printing press money to hire manual laborers to construct public works. Even this phase of infla-tion has proven illusory over the longer term, however, as the workers find their living costs mounting faster than their daily pay.

Government leaders in El Salvador are not living in a separate bureaucratic world of their own, divorced from national productive activities. Perhaps their immediate awareness of how goods are produced has shielded them from the belief that running a printing press could make the country rich. In this connection, it is interesting to note that the other countries in the hemisphere which have not devalued against the dollar in the postwar period are all of roughly the same population size as El Salvador. In larger countries, on the other hand, where individual specialization is stressed and the national economic picture may seem more obscure, government-sponsored inflation has been a normal practice despite its untoward effects.

Bearing in mind the experience in other, larger coun-tries, the future outlook for Salvadoran finance may not be entirely bright. Increased specialization in banking manage-ment and ownership may in time lead to higher lending rates throughout the country. If the banking community determines to maximize profits, it may also lower the rates paid on savings and thus snuff out incentives for those aspiring to middle-class status.

Perhaps a more imminent danger lies in the sphere of national government, since governmental policies can of themselves override actions of the private financial com-munity. There is no guarantee, beyond the common sense of the electorate, that a leader may not come to power who promises that simple fiscal and monetary manipulations will make everyone rich. As the country grows, the risks of such

oversimplified solutions probably increase, if experience in
other countries is a valid indication.   The antidote to the
inflationary drug appears to remain that which has thus far
maintained Salvadoran price stability: direct and certain
knowledge from personal observation that goods are only
produced by hard work and not by abstruse fiscal decrees.

TRADE AND
COMMERCE

El Salvador's trade and commerce move the country's exports abroad, import those essentials and luxuries the country can't itself produce, and manage the interchange of all local production made for sale. Most studies of Salvadoran trade have concentrated on the foreign component, which is clearly vital to the nation's well-being. Foreign trade, however, represents only a small portion of total national commerce. In the following analysis the foreign and domestic sectors are segregated, though few detailed figures are available regarding internal commerce.

FOREIGN TRADE

Salvadoran foreign commerce has expanded considerably in both dollar and material volume since the prewar period. In 1929, the peak year before the Depression, Salvadoran exports worth $18.4 million covered imports of $17.8 million. Sharply lower coffee prices continued through most of the 1930's. Over the three-year span 1936-38, exports averaged $13.1 million against average imports of $9.3 million. During World War II, El Salvador continued to export much more than it imported, due to the scarcity of supplies in the wartime period. In the immediate postwar period dislocations eased, and save for a 1949 drop in imports, both export and import levels increased each year through 1955.

Coffee exports in 1955, though only one-third higher in volume than in 1938, brought in ten times as much income due to favorable price changes. Enlarged coffee receipts, plus the growth of export earnings from cotton, and later shrimp, permitted continued favorable balances of export over imports until 1960. In that year there was a burst of importation, caused in the first nine months by a booming economy and then encouraged by scare buying after the 1960 revolution. For the first time in decades El Salvador had a small unfavorable balance in merchandise trade, with exports and imports each close to $120 million. A favorable trade balance was regained in the next few years.

On the export side, the major commodities in trade were coffee, cotton, shrimp, and sugar in the period under consideration. Coffee has gone principally to the United States and West Germany, cotton to Japan, shrimp to the United States, and sugar to Honduras and the United States. All of these exports earn hard currencies, and thus do not involve the country in closely balanced barter-type transactions.

The solid position of the colon currency, and the hard currency earnings of the country's exports, made it possible throughout the period for the country's importers to choose among all available world markets for their imports. The major suppliers throughout the period have been the United States, West Germany, the Netherlands (mostly petroleum products from the Netherlands Antilles), and Great Britain. In recent years, Japan has also become an important supplier. The special case of trade with other Central American countries, now almost half as large as trade with the United States, will be further discussed below.

During the long span of favorable trade balances, there were a number of ways that export proceeds could be used without converting them directly into imports. Exporters could have sales proceeds banked for them abroad, without having payment arrive in El Salvador. A proportion of exchange earnings was expended for insurance, freight, and financing charges connected with the trade itself. Proceeds from exports which arrived in the country could be kept as foreign currency (chiefly dollar) deposits in the commercial banks, or exchanged through the Central Bank for colones. Trade earnings which arrived inside the country's banking system could then be used to finance foreign travel and education, in addition to imports. Finally, any amount of exchange earnings not used in these ways was added to the international reserves of the Central Bank.

These international reserves, which built up rapidly during World War II and the immediate postwar period, added to the stability of the national currency. They also provided the basis for Salvadoran government subscriptions to various international organizations, chiefly the IMF, the IBRD, the Inter-American Development Bank, and the Central American

Development Bank. Government-secured funds were also used by the middle of the 1950's to pay interest and principal on loans from the Export-Import Bank and the IBRD, whose investments in the country had arrived in the form of imported goods.

In most rapidly developing countries, imports exceed exports by a substantial sum, as the expanding economy attracts outside funds from foreign loans, foreign investments, or both. This pattern will probably emerge during this decade in El Salvador, and the reserves built up in past years will provide a considerable cushion with which to provide foreign exchange for the eventual repayment of interest, dividends, and principal.

CENTRAL AMERICAN TRADE

Efforts toward establishing a Central American Common Market, which began to bear fruit in 1959, have created a newly important feature in the Salvadoran trading pattern. Ideally, trade within a common market should be almost as simple as domestic commerce, without the attendant difficulties and complexities associated with international trade.

A variety of institutional steps have been taken since 1959 to facilitate the transition to a common market embracing Guatemala, El Salvador, Honduras, Nicaragua, Costa Rica, and to the extent possible, Panama. The success of these efforts should not be measured in terms of written documents or diplomatic understandings, but must bear a tangible test of increased trade. The practical success of the program in the past few years is shown in Table 5.

TABLE 5

Salvadoran Trade with Central America*
(figures in $ millions)

Year	Exports	Imports	Total	% of Total Trade
1956	$ 5.2	$ 8.1	$13.3	6%
1959	10.5	12.5	23.0	11%
1962	18.7	22.1	40.8	16%

*Figures do not include trade with Panama.
SOURCE: Central Reserve Bank: Revista Mensual.

The acceleration of trade within the Central American area is fulfilling long-held aspirations of many in the area. Despite fears to the contrary, the goals of increased trade have been able to survive abrupt political changes, which have included coups-d'etat in El Salvador, Guatemala, and Honduras in the past few years. If present trends continue, as appears likely, within a few years about a quarter of Salvadoran trade should be with the neighboring Central American countries. Because the common market precepts are designed to minimize problems of tariffs, other trade restrictions, and currency payments, an increasing number of individuals will be able to participate in this trade with little more skill than is necessary in domestic commerce.

Though highly important to Salvadoran development, the creation of the Common Market will not be a panacea guaranteeing inevitable future economic growth. What the Common Market does do is to permit producers in each Central American country to have preferred access to a purchasing pool composed of a total of over 10 million people -- rather than, as in the case of El Salvador, 2.5 million people. However, the Common Market does not change two basic facts in the area. Most of the production, being agricultural, is largely similar, and hence is unlikely to be exchanged across frontiers. Perhaps more important, consumer incomes in each of the countries are generally low.

This means, to take the Salvadoran case, that access to the Common Market might increase the potential buying public for a manufacturer of medium-cost consumer goods by perhaps fourfold. Instead of, for example, a market of 50,000 people in El Salvador, he might hope to sell to 250,000 throughout Central America. Selling efficiency would have been even greater if the increase of 200,000 customers had taken place in El Salvador, due to lessened costs of transportation and marketing. Access to other Central American consumers should be regarded as a temporary bonus, permitting initial plant establishment or expansion. But long-term growth will still be dependent upon expanding purchasing power as close to the plant as possible.

DOMESTIC COMMERCE

According to Ministry of Labor estimates, about 6 percent of the economically active population is engaged in domestic commerce. This field of activity is believed to generate about 18 percent of the Gross National Product (GNP). At its most rudimentary level, commercial activity includes the barter of farm products. Somewhat more complex, because money is involved, are the small trading operations carried on by farmers and market women in the provincial market towns. Finally, in important cities and the capital, full-scale commercial operations bring domestic production and imports to the ultimate consumers.

The small numerical size of the country's middle class has to a considerable extent cramped the development of commercial enterprise. Inventory turnover tends to be low, and price markups high. Consumer credit operations, such as installment buying, are largely lacking, as are mass-selling, low-margin retail operations. In the postwar period there has been a gradual development of a few mass retailers, chiefly in the field of super markets, but much opportunity remains.

One feature of Salvadoran social psychology, which is also common elsewhere in Latin America, puts a low social premium on employment or ownership in commerce. As a rule, land ownership is the socially preferred form of wealth, with industry now perhaps taking its place. There is somewhat the same feeling about employment, with industrial employment preferred to employment in trade. Today industry and commerce together are the two main recruiting areas for entrants to the middle class, and as time passes the prejudice against commercial activity will probably decline.

CHAPTER 9   POLITICAL SUMMARY

Under various constitutions in the last hundred years, the central government has been headed by a President. There is a national legislative assembly, and a Supreme Court of Justice. The fourteen regional departments are administered by governors appointed by the executive. As a general rule the political tone of the country has been set by those controlling the executive branch.

The main political changes in the thirty years under consideration were the following:

1931:   General Maximiliano Hernández Martínez, Minister of War in the preceding government, took power in a military coup. He succeeded in putting down a widespread revolt (the sublevación) which drew considerable support from Communist-inspired leaders trained in Europe.

1944:   A coup replaced Martínez.

1945:   General Salvador Castañeda Castro took power as President.

1948:   A coup replaced Castañeda Castro. Several juntas followed.

1950:   Major Oscar Osorio, candidate of the last junta, was elected President.

1956:   Lt. Col. José María Lemus, supported by the Osorio administration, was elected President.

1960:   A coup in October replaced Lemus. A junta was installed.

1961:   A second coup in January reversed the first junta and established a second.

1962:   Lt. Col. Julio A. Rivera was elected President.

CHAPTER
10

RISKS AND COSTS IN ECONOMIC DEVELOPMENT

Rapid economic development creates a climate of unusual risks and costs, as well as opportunities for profit. Events in El Salvador during the period under consideration were no exception. Long established experience, which did not meet the new challenges of change, became for many individuals a handicap. Some in the economy probably gained by pure luck. Those most successful in the transition period, however, showed significant combinations of flexibility and foresight.

Salvadoran development did not proceed in economic isolation from the rest of the world. This survey, which is limited to a span of roughly thirty years from the depths of the world Depression to the early 1960's, covers a period in which there were massive changes in world markets. These changes in turn had inevitable impact on the decisions made by Salvadorans themselves as they conducted their own affairs.

We recall from the chapter on agriculture that throughout its history, Salvadoran agricultural exports played a key role in the economy, because exports made possible the importation of diversified products which could not be made locally. The inherent flexibility of export earnings put a premium on the key export crops. The result was that in many cases, a landholder would grow an export crop in preference to a locally consumed food crop such as corn.

In the early 1930's, when the economy was still almost entirely agricultural, land ownership as such was highly regarded. This was in keeping with traditional social values. The established value system also put a preference on export crop production when alternative land uses were considered. However, at the same point in time, the price of the principal export crop, coffee, had dropped to unprecedented lows of several cents per pound.

Coffee growers had enjoyed great economic success in the period through World War I and the 1920's. The old, established indigo export market had collapsed with the introduction of synthetic dyestuffs. Now, with the vertical drop in coffee prices, it seemed that the coffee bonanza was over. New investments in coffee land and coffee trees appeared to be rank speculation.

However, for those still making profits from commerce and not holding land, the attraction of becoming landholders and engaging in export production remained. Land prices were unusually low, and liquid capital was scarce. A new group of landholders developed, in part by buying out established coffee fincas, and in part by buying undeveloped mountain land for new planting. Meanwhile, some established coffee growers cut back their holdings as uneconomic ventures, and other established growers added to their fincas in the hope of eventual price improvement.

As coffee prices rose in World War II, those who had risked new capital in coffee investments were richly rewarded. The established growers who had remained -- some now in the second generation -- also profited from their constancy. Those who sold out at the bottom were having varying degrees of success a decade later, depending upon how the proceeds had been reinvested.

During the period that these changes took place, there were a number of alternative possibilities for the investment of new capital. Investments in land could have been directed toward food production for domestic consumption, thus driving down food prices and improving national diet levels. The risk-takers did not, in the main, adopt this course, and one of the social costs of the new investments in coffee was that the national diet remained at a subsistence level. From the risk-taker's point of view, however, the investment in coffee in time proved more profitable than an investment in corn.

Another alternative use of capital could have been for industrial investment -- probably in those same industries which were established after World War II. One important industry was established: the henequen bag operation which in turn was tied to the coffee exports. However, at a time when world industrial prices were unusually low and local demand almost stagnant, it is doubtful whether many more industrial investments would have paid off.

Following World War II, new investments continued to be made in coffee fincas as coffee prices increased. The same forces which led to new investment in coffee in the 1930's encouraged investments in the new cotton plantations. A further influence favoring cotton investments on the part of

established landholders was an effort at agricultural diversification in the export sector.

While prices continued to increase for coffee and cotton
through the Korean War and immediately thereafter, a number
of key Salvadoran entrepreneurs began making a crucial
decision to put further profits from exports into industrial
investment.

The group of individuals planning along these lines was
not particularly large, but their efforts were mutually rein-
forcing, and their success was rapid. To their advantage was
the fact that the initial industrial technologies were already
well known and established in other countries. A major difficulty was the need to establish a manpower pool capable of
operating the new industries. Perhaps even more difficult
was the problem of developing managerial talent at the level
of foreman and above.

Industrialization quickly gained prestige, due not only to
profits but also to the reflected sophistication coming from
industrial establishments. Savings of additional individuals
became oriented toward industrial investments. For the first
time on an important scale in the country, individuals invested
large sums to be cared for and managed by others. The traditional identity between owner and manager was broken, with
a consequent increase in the flexibility of capital in the country.

At the present initial stage of Salvadoran industrial
development, the steps leading to industrial investment can be
outlined roughly as follows:

1933-45:

Land profits reinvested toward land, finance, liquid assets;
Commercial profits reinvested toward commerce, land,
    finance.

1946-55:

Land profits reinvested toward land, finance, industry;
Commercial profits reinvested toward commerce, land,
    finance, industry.

1956-6-:

Land profits reinvested toward land, finance, industry;
Commercial profits reinvested toward commerce, land,
    finance, industry;
Industrial profits reinvested toward industry.

A notable feature of the outline above is that it does not show profits flowing into commerce from outside sources. While purely commercial operations are often highly profitable in the country, they carry no special social prestige such as that accruing to landholding, finance, or industry. This lack of social prestige in commercial activity probably serves to decrease potential competition in this field. It also permits relatively easy entry into commercial activity by unestablished individuals who are moving away from agricultural or industrial manual labor. Success in commerce then in turn leads to an orientation toward landholding, industrial investment, or both.

THE STRUCTURE OF RISKS

During these three decades of rapid development, there was a concentration of risk-taking in a few hands. It is normal for any individual about to embark on a new venture to seek to share the risks; but this was difficult to do in the El Salvador of the 1930's. As noted in previous chapters, liquid funds were scarce, financial institutions were small and inefficient, and the government played a negligible role in the national economy.

Formal risk-sharing was possible within a family group, or within a small group of close friends. Essentially, however, the risks associated with new investments were borne directly by individuals who risked all or a portion of the capital they had accumulated from more traditional forms of enterprise.

While the assumption of risk on this basis was feasible for investments in agriculture, and later in small industrial plants, it was not practical for projects requiring large initial capital investments, such as power production, ports, and highways. Before the period under consideration, the country's two railroads and the capital's electric utility had been financed by private foreign capital, but since then, private funds from abroad had only entered the country in small amounts.

It thus became necessary to form a combination between private local capital and government capital in the semi-autonomous organizations which financed construction of the country's large hydroelectric power project and the port facilities at Acajutla. These semi-autonomous institutions in turn were able to attract foreign capital from governmental or international lending organizations located abroad.

In the field of highway building, the government did not draw on private financing, but did attract outside financial assistance from the United States, in connection with the Inter-American Highway, and from the IBRD for the Littoral Highway and some feeder roads.   Preceding these investments, the government had already stressed highway investments in many parts of the country. As highway availabilities increased, there was a rapid buildup of road transport in the postwar period.

While in general the risk-taking during the period had fortunate results, it is worth considering the alternatives which were available to the various types of investors. Private individuals, for example, could have decided to maintain their investment patterns unchanged from the 1930's. Had this choice been made, there would probably be little change in the Salvadoran economy today from the subsistence agricultural structure of the early 1930's. Industrial concepts and organizations would be conspicuously absent. In this hypothetical situation, the risk-takers could have played it safe, but the entire economy would have suffered.

One could also ask what would have happened if the government, instead of putting its capital funds into the construction of highways, ports, power plants, and schools, had invested in farms or perhaps commerce and industry. Of the limited government funds available, there would have been less to provide each of the types of investment than actually flowed from private sources; certainly transportation and power construction would have had to be cut back in order to fund the needs of the other types of enterprises.   If the government had increased taxation in order to capture more resources, government-owned commercial enterprises would have been plagued with managerial problems, due to the frequent unscheduled changes in the government power structure. Finally, since the investors in a government operation are basically the citizens (because their taxes provide the funds), all the citizens would have been bearing the business risks which, in fact, private enterprise actually bore during the period.

In the Salvadoran case, at least, there appears to have been a minimum public risk over the medium term for funds invested in transportation and power production facilities. It is hard to imagine a case in which a road can "fail." Being there, and open to the public, a road is used. Perhaps it is not used as much as expected; or it may be unnecessarily expensive for the use developed. Still the road remains, and is used on into the future. Investments of a business type, however (farms, commercial establishments, industries) have a different type of inherent risk; frequently the investment can practically disappear, due to losses from bad management, misjudging the market, etc. Private investors continue to be attracted to this type of investment, due to the high returns paid success -- but these high returns are also in part reflecting the risks of failure.

By keeping its funds out of the business type of enterprise, the Salvadoran government was in the fortunate position that it did not need to finance business losses, and yet remained free to tax business success. So long as private investors remain willing to bear moderate risks, there appears to be no reason for the government to change this position.

BEARING THE COSTS

If we grant that, in general, the risks taken during this period were well judged and bore results, there were still costs within the national economy. The individual risk-taker who sought to make an agricultural or industrial investment had to accumulate capital somehow -- usually from profits gained from business within the country. These profits were, in a sense, his tax on the national economy, which once collected could be put into new productive investment. The risk-taker's idea of necessary profit margins affects his competitors also, and the economy may bear an additional cost by providing profits to a second individual who does not invest the gains in new productive enterprise, but instead uses the proceeds for personal consumption.

While it would appear difficult to sort out the two types of individuals, the government made some attempt in tax legislation which favored the reinvestment of farm, commercial, or industrial gross profits into new investment, as opposed to dividends. This has had some effect in putting a premium on reinvestment, but significant cases remain of individuals and groups preferring consumption to new investment.

The whole economy in general bore the costs of expanded government investments during the period. Tax payers were immediately aware of these increased charges, but even direct taxes in time are passed down throughout the economy, making it difficult to calculate just who pays how much. In general, it would appear that the burden was well diffused throughout the populace as the money economy expanded to include the entire population. Again, since the government investments on the whole appear to have had a beneficial effect, these diffused contributions to government projects appear to have been economically useful.

Because it maintained a generally sober and conservative program of public investment in the postwar period, the government was also able to attract funds from governmental and international financial institutions abroad. In effect, this meant that the savings of foreigners were invested in Salvadoran public programs, complementing local tax resources. The terms of the foreign borrowings were not onorous, and the direct economic benefits of the resulting projects were such as to generate more than enough funds for scheduled repayments.

REFLECTIONS ON THE SALVADORAN EXPERIENCE

THE MYSTERIOUS PAST

The simplified record of Salvadoran economic growth in the past three decades shows that population roughly doubled, and production increased even more than twofold. With hindsight, there is a temptation to picture this development as an orderly process. However, at no time did the leaders in the national economy make their plans with certainty concerning the future -- no one knew for sure how the experience in the three decades would turn out. From our perspective, what helpful generalizations can be made about the past? Several observations appear to be useful.

Initially, we have noted that most of the decisions of importance in the Salvadoran economy have been made by a relatively small number of people. The potential decision-making base for a population the size of El Salvador can be outlined like this:

Total population	2,500,000
subtract: those under 15	-1,000,000
subtract: women over 15*	- 750,000
Remaining male* base, over 15	750,000

Clearly it would not be possible for the entire male population over 15 years old to share equally in economic decisions. In the first place, many are illiterate. Secondly, many are not qualified, due to lack of work experience. Finally, some who

---

*This is shorthand. Actually, there are some thousands of women -- chiefly full-time market women in the larger cities -- who are very important economically. Also, of course there are some men over 15 who make no economic contribution to speak of.

might be qualified in other terms can not exercise decisive influence because they are not in the strategic positions where economic decisions are made.

If there are to be leaders, there must also be followers. It might be possible to imagine a ratio of one leader to nine followers in an extremely open society. Applying this to the Salvadoran figures, this would provide 75,000 leaders and 675,000 followers. Actually, power is held in fewer hands -- perhaps between 1 and 3 percent of the population group, rather than 10 percent. Since the economy was opening up and becoming less restrictive during the period under consideration, it might be possible as an approximation to say that 1 percent of the male population over 15 years old was making important economic decisions in the early 1930's, and 3 percent of this group by the early 1960's. In round numbers this would be:

> 4,000 decisive males in the early 1930's (1 percent of the male base over 15, or 375,000);
> 24,000 decisive males in the early 1960's (3 percent of the male base over 15, or 750,000).

These calculations have been made on a basis of the national population alone. During the period under discussion, foreign investments were largely limited to the two railroads and the power company in the capital, and few new investments were made. Foreign aid and assistance was limited in scope except toward the close of the period. Because of these limitations, the effects of foreign decision-makers were less than in many other countries at the same time. For the most part, those few foreigners who played decisive roles in the development of the economy were in the country as hired managers, and thus directly subordinate to Salvadoran individuals or groups.

We can go further than just noting that decisions were made by relatively few men. Examination of the past three decades shows that these key individuals were organized or interrelated in a pattern which reflected the productive nature of the economy: agriculture, commerce, finance, and later industry. Few were in government. The government's role in the national economy at the start of the period was slight, and in the postwar period, much of the government's participation came through the semi-autonomous institutions such as the Lempa River Power Authority (CEL).

Because major economic decisions were not centralized in the national government, the several revolutionary political changes which actually took place, and other attempts which failed, had less economic effect than would have been the case had the government controlled most economic change. Naturally these political changes were not without their impact, but the effects were limited due to the alignment of economic decision-makers outside the government apparatus.

As a final generalization, it would appear that the decisive men in the Salvadoran economy have been essentially tolerant in their behavior. The number of men actually making decisions seems to have increased much faster than the population as a whole. This indicates that the system is not closed to new entrants, but rather that, as the economy expands and becomes more complex, even larger opportunities will open up to those not yet participating at the decision level.

THE UNKNOWN FUTURE

If we had studied the Salvadoran economy a generation ago, and had for our perspective a complete and objective view of it during the three decades of 1900-30, it seems unlikely that this knowledge would have equipped us to predict the surprising changes which actually took place in the next thirty years. It is more likely that we would have predicted a continuation of the then-present situation: a more-or-less self-sufficient agricultural economy supporting a stable population at low levels of consumption.

Likewise, with the experience of the past three decades in mind, predictions of the future are naturally tied to recent experience, and involve increasing industrialization, a growing population, and further improvements in education and skills. It is possible that such a predictive framework could be just as wrong as the most logical predictions made in the early 1930's, because the future rarely turns out to be merely a continuation of past trends.

This is not to say that perspective has no advantages at all. The identification of a current trend can assist evaluation of the future along two lines of development: with the trend, or with a major deviation from the trend. If the economy develops along present lines for an additional period of time, it is possible to make rough descriptive predictions of its appearance in the future. On the other hand, if the present trend is cut off and a new trend develops, we can anticipate in advance that such a change in direction would create major internal conflicts in the Salvadoran economy.

Potential new trends deserve some examination, though they seem less likely on the evidence than a continuation along present lines. One possibility, which can be described with some accuracy since it has been experienced in other countries, would be that the national government became the decisive force in the Salvadoran economy. We have noted that of the roughly 24,000 decision-makers now active nationally, few are in government service -- probably less than 10 percent. It is possible to imagine a situation in which the populace would acquiesce in centralizing economic decisions in a government bureaucracy, though this would mean a major change.

Most of the decision-makers presently operating in a framework of private enterprise or connected with the semi-autonomous institutions would find it difficult to change their methods of operation. Furthermore, in most economies where the national government has taken the central role, few individuals who were established in the previous economic system have been invited to participate. Projecting such a possibility in El Salvador, the likelihood would be that while many of the present 24,000 would be stripped of their effective powers, a new group, assimilated somehow under the governmental aegis, would take over decisive economic responsibilities.

Such a group would have, as working assets, the taxing and regulatory powers of the state. To effectively replace the present productivity of the current system, both taxes and regulations would have to increase considerably from present levels to give the new decision-makers sufficient assets with which to work. As intellectual capital, the potential new leaders would not have decision-making experience as such (recalling that those who had such experience would be largely excluded from participation on various grounds); but in all probability this lack would be glossed over by reliance on a doctrinal approach. Most current doctrine in this field traces back to Marxist origins, so that a potential Salvadoran adaptation would probably be socialistic or Communistic in nature.

Such a regime, if paternally socialistic, might receive considerable popular support and hold power even through a drop in economic progress. A Communist state, on the other hand, maintains its power through open coercion, and need not worry too much about popular consent. Under either type of centralized control, basic changes would be almost certain. In a country still largely agricultural in its values, such a government would seek to apply doctrine to the agricultural field. In the plantation-type crops (i.e., coffee, sugar, cotton), where large holdings are most efficient and day labor essential at peak periods, the government could either pass through the chaos of splitting up the holdings into tiny, inefficient units, or else nationalize the large holdings as they were, converting the agricultural labor force to government employment.   Agricultural strikes would become revolutionary attempts against the state, and probably punished as such. Whether or not there would be a gain in production is doubtful; certainly experience in Communist-directed societies has shown repeated agricultural failures for the past half century.

Central regulation of commerce, finance, and industry by a new group of decision-makers would likewise involve a period of intensive readjustment.   In other countries, such a transition period has been glossed over by a deliberate inflationary program.   Inflation on a large scale has the effect of wiping out the old middle class (the previous decision-makers now excluded from power), while rendering the rest of the population more docile because it is bemused by the money illusion.   Inflation when practiced long enough begins to operate like the distorting mirrors at a carnival -- productive enterprises lose their attractiveness, and wasteful practices appear profitable.   Through the transition period, though total production drops, the physical appearance of newly printed money conceals the productive depression and leads many to think that progress is actually being achieved.

Fortunately, the transition to a bleak, doctrinaire state does not appear to be the most likely development in the Salvadoran economy.   It has been described as an alternative to a continuation of the present trend to point up the fact that the future is not certain.

A more likely development of the Salvadoran economy would build upon many elements now active throughout the republic.   Essential features would be an expansion of the capital to a city holding a million people or more, further gains in agricultural production, and very large increases in commerce and industry. Government investments in education, transportation facilities, and communication would necessarily increase.   Per-capita incomes would show a gradual increase, but more importantly, the range of individual opportunities would increase sharply.

A twenty-year continuation of present tendencies would have the effect, in most fields, of increasing production at least twofold. A likely range would include the following features:

TABLE 6

Twenty-Year Projections of the Economy

	Expansion level from 1960
● population of the country:	x 1.5
● population of the capital:	x 3
● literate population:	x 3
● coffee production:	x 1.3
● sugar production:	x 3
● cotton production:	x 3
● corn production:	x 3
● cattle production:	x 3
● industrial production:	x 5
● government income/expenditures:	x 3
● international trade:	x 2
of which Central American Common Market trade:	x 4
● Gross National Product (GNP):	x 2
● GNP per capita:	x 1.3

There is nothing certain about this projection, but it appears possible in terms of the potential of the present Salvadoran economy. Development along these lines would not satisfy everyone in the country; much would remain to be done. For those participating in the country's development, progress would continue to be slow, grueling work, not without occasional deviations from the desired goals. But in a country which dreams of economic progress, a further part of the dream would be fulfilled.

CHAPTER 12   GENERAL OBSERVATIONS ON PROTEAN ECONOMIES

We are all impressed by the explosive capabilities natural scientists have achieved by study and experimentation in the last hundred years. Those who study human social phenomena (historians, economists, etc.) often seek to give a scientific cast to their work, in order to improve their capacity to make predictions. While results have not been as precise as in the natural sciences, still this effort goes on.

In this context it is fair to ask whether a general theory can be devised, which would account for economic development in all societies, regardless of how organized, and regardless of time frame. If this does not prove possible, perhaps more limited theories accounting for a portion of the societies might be devised.

There are about 3 billion people in the world at this time. Most of the economic information about people is organized by nationality, so it is useful to note the largest national units.

TABLE 7

Largest National Units by Population (1960)

China (Mainland)	700 million
India	425 million
U.S.S.R.	215 million
U.S.A.	180 million
Japan	94 million
Pakistan	90 million
Indonesia	90 million
	1,794 million

In just these seven national units, about 60 percent of the world's population lives.

A table of the most productive national units would contain some different entries, because sheer population magnitude has not necessarily brought prosperity.

TABLE 8

Largest Productive Units, Early 1960's

U.S.A.	$ 585 billion
U.S.S.R.	200 billion
United Kingdom	83 billion
West Germany	80 billion
France	75 billion
China (Mainland)	63 billion
Japan	60 billion
	$1,146 billion

These seven national units account for about 70 percent of all economic production in the entire world.

Thus far the search for a general theory of development has not been too successful with the largest population units. It is hard to fit experiences as diverse as those in India, the U. S. S. R. , and the United States into the same formulation. In recent years there has been more success in dealing with the large productive aggregates, particularly the United States, leading Western European countries, and Japan.

In the case of the large productive units, the data (steel mills, highways, cities) have been generally homogeneous, simplifying description. Development in the leading countries has been largely contemporaneous and interacting, leading to further simplifications. The theory based on these studies, however, has had to discard a large number of nations from immediate consideration, under the catch-all term of "underdeveloped." A more optimistic formulation in terms of stages of economic growth picks up developing economies at a productive level of from $10 to $20 billion as a "take-off" point.

Many of the world's economic units, however, are still left in an "underdeveloped" or "pre-take-off" limbo. Economists hesitate to predict their development process until they become more like the known, bigger economies. The smaller, less certain economies remain as protean elements in international economic analysis.

PROTEAN ECONOMIES AND THE DIVISION OF LABOR

Political economists two centuries ago recognized that economic progress is closely linked with the advantages to be gained from a division of labor. The division of labor, in turn, is necessarily influenced by population size. Great Britain, the first country to develop rapidly in the industrial revolution, was in part a natural leader because its eighteenth century population of 7 million made it one of the largest national units in the world at that time.

The smaller protean economies today are those where the division of labor has not yet taken decisive form. Most of the economically active population is engaged in agriculture, though there is a strong popular ambition for more diversified economic activity. Because population totals are relatively low, even agriculture is not totally institutionalized. Innovations introduced by just a handful of entrepreneurs can lead to major changes in the economy.

It may prove possible to develop a method of approach which could apply in a systematic way to these protean economies. These economies appear to have a population of six million people or less. Units smaller than 1 million people have been left out of this survey, not because they are not protean, but because of the difficulties in securing comparable data. These small economies are listed in Appendix II. Population units larger than 6 million people have been set aside on the theory that as populations enlarge, so do institutional practices. Growing institutional inertia, in turn, leads toward economic crystallization, the reverse of the disorganized flexibility in a protean economy. The economies with populations between 6 and 10 million people are listed in Appendix III.

Of the fifty-three geographic units with a population size between 1 and 6 million in 1960 (Appendix I), fifty-one can be compared. Singapore and Hong Kong have been dropped from further comparisons because they are essentially urban.

Forty-nine of the remaining fifty-one are independent countries, so that this group contains about 40 percent of all the countries in the world. These fifty-one units contain about 5 percent of the world's population: a magnitude about as large as the combined population of West Germany, the United Kingdom, and France, or three-quarters the population of the United States.

In production terms, each of the units has production (Gross National Product) of about $100 million or more annually, but none produces as much as $10 billion. Total annual production for the group appears to be about $49 billion, which is about 3 percent of world production. GNP levels are set out in Appendixes IX to XIII.

Present production levels in the group are about equal to the increase in American GNP over a one-year period. While a further one-year development of the American economy will not produce many major surprises, it is difficult to say today what the fifty-one protean economies will be like when their total production has expanded by an additional $50 billion. Certainly, in many instances the entire national flavor and thrust will have changed.

Geographically these economies are extremely scattered. Thirteen are in the Western Hemisphere, twenty-three in Africa, six in Europe, and the remaining nine in the Middle East, Asia, and Oceania (see Appendix IV). In political terms, thirty-one of the fifty-one were not independent at the end of World War II (see Appendix VIII).

A single economy's development is largely a function of its past performance and present expectations. However, at a given point in time it is also possible to measure performance against the maximum uses human beings have been able to draw from specific levels of resources. For example, we may know that today the production of Country X, with its population of 2 million, is on the order of $100 million annually. It is useful to see that at the present time the greatest known production level for a nation of 2 million is in country Y, at a level twenty-five times greater.

This kind of approach would limit economic projections for protean economies as much as possible to known, actual achievements in other protean economies at a given point in time. Conjecture would still enter into the analysis, since there are difficulties in determining which leading countries should be picked as guideposts for the country under discussion. The conjectural problem appears to be the greatest for economies which are already leading, while posing fewer problems for those which are lagging.

It is not intended here to provide more than a sketch of the possibilities of this approach. It has been used in the chapter outlining possible courses for Salvadoran economic development, where the predictive aspects were based not only on known developments in the recent Salvadoran past, but also on the known possibilities for smaller countries in the 1960's.

As an application of the method to larger bodies of data, however, it may be worth while putting the following questions to the data for the fifty-one geographic units tabulated in the Appendixes:

> Which geographic units will enter or leave the group by 1980?

> Which units will have the largest production in their geographic area by 1980?

The first question requires a projection of population changes over time. A rate of 2 percent growth compounded over twenty years would move the West Indies Federation, Basutoland, Bhutan, Trinidad and Tobago, Congo (Brazzaville), Mauritania, Mongolia, and the Ryukyu Islands into the category of geographic units with a population of a bit over 1 million. Meanwhile, the same moderate rate of population growth would move Cambodia, the Malagasy Republic, and Switzerland out of the group, since their populations would rise to over 6 million.

Examining the potential productive levels in 1980, none of the smaller countries entering the group appear to have the near-term potential to assume productive leadership.

Among the thirteen Western Hemisphere units in the group at present, the productive leaders are Uruguay, $1.4 billion; the Dominican Republic and Ecuador, each at $800 million; Jamaica and Guatemala, each at $700 million; and El Salvador, at $500 million. Uruguay will probably lead the group in 1980, though the lead is likely to narrow due to a chronic lack of dynamism in the economy. The Dominican Republic, Jamaica, and El Salvador, not having to overcome barriers of divisive languages and cultures within their borders (see Appendix VI), probably will advance faster than Ecuador and Guatemala. The 1980 picture might show Salvadoran production close to $1 billion, production in Jamaica and the Dominican Republic a bit higher, and production in Uruguay at a level of about $1.75 billion.

Of the twenty-three African units, economic leadership is at present held by Tunisia, followed by Senegal, the Ivory Coast, the Malagasy Republic, and the Cameroons. Massive oil development in Libya appears likely to move that country into a leadership position too by 1980. The 1980 picture would probably show Tunisia still leading, at a productive level of a bit over $1 billion, with Senegal and Libya each producing close to $1 billion.

Among the five remaining European countries in 1980 with a population of between 1 and 6 million, Denmark would probably retain leadership, with a GNP of over $10 billion. Rapid economic growth might bring Ireland closer to Norway and Finland than it is today. Albania, the only communist country in the present list of fifty-one, would still lag far behind the other European countries.

Finally, among the nine countries in the Middle East, Asia, and Oceania, special factors quite clearly affect the position of each country. New Zealand, Israel, and Lebanon appear to be the best situated for further rapid growth. The latter could reach a productive level of $1 billion by 1980, while the other two would still be far ahead.

In tabular form, these projections can be summarized as follows:

TABLE 9

Projected Economic Leaders, 1980

	Annual GNP
Senegal	close to $1 billion
Libya	close to $1 billion
El Salvador	close to $1 billion
Lebanon	over $1 billion
Dominican Republic	over $1 billion
Jamaica	over $1 billion
Tunisia	over $1 billion
Uruguay	$1.75 billion
Ireland	3 billion
Israel	4 billion
New Zealand	6 billion
Norway	7 billion
Finland	7 billion
Denmark	over $10 billion

THE DANGER OF AGGREGATES

Statistical materials are limited and inaccurate in most of the fifty-one economic units under discussion. As one census director put it, "Why be accurate about poverty?"

The doubtful nature of the figures makes detailed analysis difficult; especially so for analysis based on the largest aggregates, such as Gross National Product (GNP).

Our analytic problems are further complicated by the lack of competent people to make extensive analysis. It is highly doubtful that there are, in more than a few of the fifty-one geographic units under consideration, more than fifty individuals who have an effective operative knowledge of the entire economy. Of this small number of individuals, a handful may be foreigners resident in the country, and another handful barred from immediate usefulness due to the workings of local politics. Even to mention a number like fifty invites derision, since in some of the economic units it is doubtful that one-tenth that number exists.

Within the practical limits set by lack of information and lack of individuals competent to deal with or develop large aggregates of information, the wiser course would seem to be a concentration on more comprehensible features of the economy. Here too, useful approaches may be learned by making international comparisons with other countries of roughly the same population size.

As an indication of this approach, consider for a moment the problem of city building in one of the smaller countries. If national leaders took as their models some of the largest cities in the world, they would set themselves impossible goals. A more sensible approach to city building in mid-century might put more emphasis on the work presently going on in some of the other smaller countries. Appendix V shows that among the fifty-one units under discussion, there are ten with a city containing half a million people or more. Montevideo and Copenhagen are the largest, each with a size of about 1.2 million.

One of the distinctive features of these cities, and perhaps all large cities in general, is that they are really a cluster of sub-cities or sections. This is an important feature to bear in mind when planning transportation facilities, because while almost everyone may wish to visit certain sites frequently (a business district, an amusement park), there is not much cross travel between different residential districts. Thus public investment can be concentrated on major transport arteries, like spokes of a wheel, with occasional large rim-roads, leaving it to private initiative to traverse narrower streets for which there is less demand.

A large city must also have effective communications with its hinterland. The essentials nowadays appear to be radio and television, telephone and teletype, roads and airways. All of these networks are expensive to establish and maintain, but their absence inhibits city growth and their presence accelerates it.

Another sample of this inter-country approach can be seen in the field of education.   Modern production levels appear to have considerable linkage with the educational level of the national population.   It is probably possible to produce a literate individual for about $1000 in most of these smaller countries, estimating annual costs of food, shelter, clothing, and education at around $300 for three years.   A minimum pool of literacy on the order of 100,000 people would seem necessary for the rudiments of a modern economy, giving an educational cost of $100 million for the basic pool. For those countries lacking even this minimum, education may prove to be one of the highest priority items in national plans.

A NOTE OF OPTIMISM

Those concerned with the economic future of the protean economies, be they citizens of the country involved or interested foreigners, run the normal risk of shortsighted focus on the immediate problems which concern them.   Too often, the task of development appears hopeless, particularly over the short term.

A bit of perspective would remind us that actually, few major human developments have taken place over the short term.   Our pace of accomplishment is much slower than the rapidity of desire. It is perhaps too easy to conceive a major advance, certainly much too easy to promise it for political advantage, and always hard and time-consuming to bring it about.

As suggested previously, one of the factors inhibiting growth in the protean economies is the relative absence of a division of labor.   Many of the efficiencies which could come with specialization are lacking, in part due to the limits of available educated population.   A program oriented toward increased growth would stress education and, in turn, specialization.

At the present stage of comparatively undifferentiated life in the smaller countries, however, there are important human benefits which should not be forgotten.   The fifty-one geographic units have a population total of about 150 million people, and of these, perhaps about 10 percent, or 15 million, lead rich and varied economic lives. Due to the small scale of the economies in which they live, some men are able to enjoy the challenges and rewards of several specialties which, in larger economies, are separate professions. Life has not yet become bureaucratic and institutionalized in most of the smaller countries, and so a banker can also be a farmer, a trader also a politician, a lawyer also a teacher. It is not certain that in the United States plus Canada (population about 210 million) or in Western Europe (population about 330 million), many more than 15 million individuals enjoy equally wide opportunities. In other large national aggregates of population, like mainland China, India, and the U.S.S.R., it appears certain that the proportion of those leading a rich and varied economic life, as well as the absolute number, is less than in the smaller units under consideration.

The possibilities for variety in human life should be given proper weight in evaluating the prospects for the future. Political instability, one of the forms which this variety often takes, may not be an insurmountable obstacle to human development in a small economy, though it could prove disastrous in an economic unit as large as the United States. In the protean economies, the generally slow workings of development may still proceed, with minor adjustments to reflect political change. The insulation of economic life from political surface eddies in part would seem due to the fact that many of the smaller economies are not yet integrated within their geographic frontiers. Hence the national political machinery does not yet really involve the entire populace.

Because the individual can be comparatively more important in a smaller economy than in a larger one, the possibilities for innovation and surprise may also be greater. In the larger economies, innovation is becoming an almost routinized function, budgeted as research and development. In the protean economies, foreign technologies can be imported, while the possibilities of local innovation still remain.

Taking together the factors encouraging and discouraging economic growth in the smaller countries, the future prospects appear good if measured against reasonable objectives. In national aggregate or on a per-capita basis, it is unlikely that many of the smaller economies will produce at the levels of one of the leading industrial countries in the next few decades. However, for the human participants in this adventure, life in one of the protean economies may be just as rewarding as in one of the most advanced industrial nations.

APPENDIXES

Geographic Entities with 1960 Populations of Between
1 and 6 Million (rounded to the nearest 100,000)

I

Panama*	1.1	Malawi* (former Nyasaland)	2.8
Costa Rica*	1.2	Ireland*	2.8
Libya*	1.2	Niger*	2.9
Central African Republic*	1.2		
Togo*	1.4	Dominican Republic*	3.1
New Guinea (Australia)	1.4	Guinea*	3.1
Nicaragua*	1.5	Senegal*	3.1
Jamaica*	1.6	Hong Kong	3.1
Albania*	1.6	Ivory Coast*	3.2
Lebanon*	1.6	Bolivia*	3.5
Singapore*	1.6	Southern Rhodesia	3.6
Jordan*	1.7	Upper Volta*	3.6
Honduras*	1.8	Norway*	3.6
Paraguay*	1.8	Guatemala*	3.8
Laos*	1.8		
Dahomey*	1.9	Cameroon*	4.1
		Mali*	4.1
Somalia*	2.0	Haiti*	4.2
Israel*	2.1	Tunisia*	4.2
Burundi*	2.2	Finland*	4.4
Zambia* (former Northern		Ecuador*	4.5
Rhodesia)	2.4	Angola	4.6
New Zealand*	2.4	Denmark*	4.6
EL SALVADOR*	2.5	Syria*	4.6
Liberia*	2.5		
Sierra Leone*	2.5	Yemen*	5.0
Chad*	2.7	Cambodia*	5.0
Rwanda*	2.7	Malagasy Republic*	5.4
Uruguay*	2.8	Switzerland	5.4

NOTES: Members of the United Nations in 1964 are starred *.
Countries with roughly the same population are listed in the geographic order: Western Hemisphere, Africa, Europe, all others.

SOURCES: United Nations, Monthly Bulletin of Statistics; The
World Almanac, 1964.

APPENDIX

II

Bermuda	0.1	Luxembourg*	0.3
Bahamas	0.1	Malta*	0.3
British Honduras	0.1	Reunion (Fr.)	0.3
French Guiana	0.1	Kuwait*	0.3
San Tome and Principe			
(Portugal)	0.1	Fiji	0.4
French Somaliland	0.1	North Borneo	0.4
Bahrein	0.1		
Maldive Islands	0.1	Gabon*	0.5
Seychelles	0.1	Portuguese Guinea	0.5
Brunei	0.1	South West Africa	0.5
Tonga	0.1	Papua	0.5
French Polynesia	0.1	Portuguese Timor	0.5
New Caledonia (Fr.)	0.1		
Samoa	0.1	British Guiana	0.6
		Cyprus*	0.6
Dutch West Indies	0.2	Mauritius	0.6
Iceland*	0.2		
Comoro Islands (Fr.)	0.2	West Indies Federation	
Cape Verde Islands	0.2	(Barbados, etc.)	0.7
Aden	0.2	Basutoland	0.7
Macao	0.2	Bhutan	0.7
British Solomon Islands	0.2	Sarawak* (now part of	
		Malaysia)	0.7
Guadeloupe (Fr.)	0.3		
Martinique	0.3	Trinidad and Tobago*	0.8
Surinam (Dutch)	0.3	Congo (Brazzaville)*	0.8
Bechuanaland	0.3	Mauritania*	0.8
Gambia*	0.3	Mongolia*	0.8
Swaziland	0.3		
Zanzibar* (now part of		Ryukyu Islands	0.9
Tanzania)	0.3		

NOTE: Members of the United Nations in 1964 are starred *.

SOURCES: United Nations, <u>Monthly Bulletin of Statistics; The
World Almanac,</u> 1964.

Geographic Entities with 1960 Populations of Between
6 and 10 Million (rounded to the nearest 100,000)

Mozambique	6.5
Iraq*	6.6
Uganda*	6.7
Cuba*	6.8
Ghana*	6.8
Malaysia*	6.9
Austria*	7.1
Kenya*	7.1
Venezuela*	7.4
Chile*	7.4
Saudi Arabia*	7.5
Sweden*	7.5
Bulgaria*	7.9
Greece*	8.3
Portugal*	8.8
Tanganyika* (now part of Tanzania)	9.2
Belgium*	9.2
Nepal*	9.2
Hungary*	9.9
Ceylon*	9.9

NOTE: Members of the United Nations in 1964 are starred *.

SOURCES: United Nations, <u>Monthly Bulletin of Statistics</u>; <u>The World Almanac</u>, 1964.

APPENDIX

IV

Popula-tion	Western Hemisphere	Africa	Europe	Middle East, Asia, Oceania
1.1	Panama			
1.2	Costa Rica	Libya, Central African Republic		
1.4		Togo		New Guinea (Aust.)
1.5	Nicaragua			
1.6	Jamaica		Albania	Lebanon
1.7				Jordan
1.8	Honduras, Paraguay			Laos
1.9		Dahomey		
2.0		Somalia		
2.1				Israel
2.2		Burundi		
2.4		Zambia		New Zealand
2.5	EL SALVADOR	Liberia, Sierra Leone		
2.7		Chad, Rwanda		
2.8	Uruguay	Malawi	Ireland	
2.9		Niger		
3.1	Dominican Republic	Guinea, Senegal		
3.2		Ivory Coast		
3.5	Bolivia			
3.6		Southern Rhodesia, Upper Volta	Norway	
3.8	Guatemala			
4.1		Cameroon, Mali		
4.2	Haiti	Tunisia		
4.4			Finland	
4.5	Ecuador			
4.6		Angola	Denmark	Syria
5.0				Yemen, Cambodia
5.4		Malagasy Republic	Switzerland	

SOURCE: From Appendix I.

Large Cities in the Protean Economies
(rounded to the nearest 100,000)

— QUERY: Are there one or more cities in the territory with a population of 500,000 or more?

Yes	No
	Panama
	Costa Rica
	Libya
	Central African Republic
	Togo
	Nicaragua
	Jamaica
Lebanon (Beirut, 0.5)	Albania
	Jordan
	Honduras
	Paraguay
	Laos
	Dahomey
	Somalia
	Israel
	Burundi
New Zealand (Auckland, 0.5)	Zambia
	EL SALVADOR
	Liberia
	Sierra Leone
	Chad
	Rwanda
Uruguay (Montevideo, 1.2)	Malawi
Ireland (Dublin, 0.5)	Niger
	Dominican Republic
	Guinea
	Senegal
	Ivory Coast
	Bolivia
Norway (Oslo, 0.5)	Southern Rhodesia
	Upper Volta
	Guatemala
	Cameroon
	Mali
Tunisia (Tunis, 0.7)	Haiti
Finland (Helsinki, 0.5)	
	Ecuador
Denmark (Copenhagen, 1.2)	Angola
Syria (Damascus, 0.5)	
Cambodia (Phnom-Penh, 0.6)	Yemen
	Malagasy Republic
	Switzerland

SOURCE: The World Almanac, 1964.

APPENDIX

VI

— QUERY: Do 90% or more of the adult population speak a single common language?

Yes	No
	Panama
Costa Rica	Libya
	Central African Republic
	Togo
Nicaragua	New Guinea (Australia)
Jamaica	
Albania	Lebanon
	Jordan
Honduras	Paraguay
	Laos
	Dahomey
	Somalia
	Israel
	Burundi
	Zambia
New Zealand	
EL SALVADOR	Liberia
	Sierra Leone
	Chad
	Rwanda
Uruguay	Malawi
Ireland	Niger
Dominican Republic	Guinea
	Senegal
	Ivory Coast
	Bolivia
	Southern Rhodesia
Norway	Upper Volta
	Guatemala
	Cameroon
	Mali
Haiti	Tunisia
Finland	
	Ecuador
Denmark	Angola
	Syria
	Cambodia
	Yemen
	Malagasy Republic
	Switzerland

Protean Economies Independent before 1900

— QUERY: Did the territory gain present independence before 1900?

Yes	No
	Panama
Costa Rica	Libya
	Central African Republic
	New Guinea (Australia)
	Togo
Nicaragua	
	Jamaica
	Albania
	Lebanon
	Jordan
Honduras	Laos
Paraguay	
	Dahomey
	Somalia
	Israel
	Burundi
	Zambia
	New Zealand
EL SALVADOR	
Liberia	Sierra Leone
	Chad
	Rwanda
Uruguay	Malawi
	Ireland
	Niger
Dominican Republic	Guinea
	Senegal
	Ivory Coast
Bolivia	Southern Rhodesia
	Norway
	Upper Volta
Guatemala	
	Cameroon
	Mali
Haiti	Tunisia
	Finland
Ecuador	
Denmark	Angola
	Syria
	Yemen
	Cambodia
Switzerland	Malagasy Republic

117

APPENDIX

VIII

Protean Economies Independent before 1945

— QUERY: Did the territory gain present independence before 1945?

Yes	No
Panama	
Costa Rica	Libya
	Central African Republic
	New Guinea (Australia)
	Togo
Nicaragua	
Albania	
	Jamaica
	Lebanon
	Jordan
Honduras	
Paraguay	Laos
	Dahomey
	Somalia
	Israel
	Burundi
New Zealand	Zambia
EL SALVADOR	Sierra Leone
Liberia	
	Chad
	Rwanda
Uruguay	Malawi
Ireland	
	Niger
Dominican Republic	Guinea
	Senegal
	Ivory Coast
Bolivia	
Norway	Southern Rhodesia
	Upper Volta
Guatemala	
	Cameroon
	Mali
Haiti	Tunisia
Finland	
Ecuador	
Denmark	Angola
	Syria
	Yemen
	Cambodia
Switzerland	Malagasy Republic

118

The 51 Protean Economies, Ranked within Geographic
Regions by Gross National Product
(to the nearest $100 million)

GNP	Western Hemisphere	Africa	Europe	Middle East, Asia, Oceania
$100		Central African Republic Chad Malawi Niger Dahomey Somalia Togo Zambia		Laos New Guinea (Australia)
$200	Bolivia Paraguay	Burundi Guinea Liberia Libya Mali Rwanda Sierra Leone Upper Volta		Yemen
$300	Haiti Nicaragua	Cameroon	Albania	Jordan
$400	Costa Rica Honduras Panama	Malagasy Republic		
$500	EL SALVADOR	Ivory Coast Senegal		
$600				Cambodia
$700	Guatemala Jamaica	Tunisia		Lebanon
$800	Dominican Republic Ecuador			Syria
$1400	Uruguay			
$2000			Ireland	
$2700				Israel
$4000				New Zealand
$5000			Norway	
$5300			Finland	
$7500			Denmark	
$9500			Switzerland	

SOURCES: Combination of Appendixes X through XIII.

APPENDIX

X

Population (to nearest 100,000)		Gross National Product (to nearest $100 million)	
1.1	Panama		
1.2	Costa Rica		
1.5	Nicaragua		
1.6	Jamaica	Bolivia, Paraguay	$200
1.8	Honduras, Paraguay	Haiti, Nicaragua	$300
		Costa Rica, Honduras,	$400
2.5	EL SALVADOR	Panama	
2.8	Uruguay	EL SALVADOR	$500
3.1	Dominican Republic		
		Guatemala, Jamaica	$700
3.5	Bolivia		
3.8	Guatemala	Dominican Republic, Ecuador	$800
4.2	Haiti		
4.5	Ecuador		
		Uruguay	$1400

SOURCES: Column 1 from Appendix I; Column 2 from U.S. News and World Report of December 14, 1964, in turn from United Nations and U.S. Department of State data.

Comparative Population and Gross National Product in Africa

Population (to nearest 100,000)		Gross National Product (to nearest $100 million)	
		Central African Republic, Chad, Malawi, Niger, Dahomey, Somalia, Togo, Zambia	$100
1.2	Libya, Central African Republic		
1.4	Togo		
1.9	Dahomey	Burundi, Guinea, Liberia, Libya, Mali, Rwanda, Sierra Leone, Upper Volta	$200
2.0	Somalia		
2.2	Burundi		
2.4	Zambia		
2.5	Liberia, Sierra Leone	Cameroon	$300
2.7	Chad, Rwanda	Malagasy Republic	$400
2.8	Malawi	Ivory Coast, Senegal	$500
2.9	Niger		
3.1	Guinea, Senegal		
3.2	Ivory Coast	Tunisia	$700
3.6	Southern Rhodesia, Upper Volta		
4.1	Cameroon, Mali		
4.2	Tunisia		
4.6	Angola		
5.5	Malagasy Republic		

SOURCES: Column 1 from Appendix I; Column 2 from <u>U.S. News and World Report</u> of December 14, 1964, in turn from United Nations and U.S. Department of State data. GNP of Dahomey adjusted by author.

APPENDIX

XII

Population (to nearest 100,000)		Gross National Product (to nearest $100 million)	
1.6	Albania		
2.8	Ireland		
3.6	Norway	Albania	$300
4.4	Finland		
4.6	Denmark		
5.5	Switzerland		
		Ireland	$2000
		Norway	$5000
		Finland	$5300
		Denmark	$7500
		Switzerland	$9500

SOURCES: Column 1 from Appendix I; Column 2 from U.S. News and World Report of December 14, 1964, in turn from United Nations and U.S. Department of State data. Swiss figures from The Americana Annual, 1964.

Comparative Population and Gross National Product
in the Middle East, Asia, and Oceania

Population (to nearest 100,000)		Gross National Product (to nearest $100 million)	
		New Guinea (Australia)	$100
		Laos	
1.4	New Guinea (Australia)	Yemen	$200
1.6	Lebanon		
1.7	Jordan		
1.8	Laos		
2.1	Israel		
		Jordan	$300
2.4	New Zealand		
		Cambodia	$600
		Lebanon	$700
		Syria	$800
4.6	Syria		
5.0	Yemen, Cambodia	Israel	$2700
		New Zealand	$4000

SOURCES: Column 1 from Appendix I; Column 2 from U.S. News and World Report of December 14, 1964, in turn from United Nations and U.S. Department of State data.

APPENDIX

XIV

Evolution of Population in Selected Populous Countries

Past Date at Which Population Was 6 million or less	Recent (1960/61) Population, in Millions
1700: Great Britain, less Eire: about 6 million	52.7
1750: Mexico: about 6 million	36.1
1800: United States: 5.3 million	183.3
Brazil: 3.3 million	70.8
1850: Belgium: 4.3 million	9.1
Egypt: 4.5 million	26.6
1900: Sweden: 5.1 million	7.4
Netherlands: 5.1 million	11.4
Turkey: 6 million	28.6
Canada: 5.4 million	18.2
Argentina: 4 million	21.1
Algeria: 4.7 million	11.1
Australia: 3.8 million	10.5
1920: Morocco: 4.3 million	11.9

SOURCES: QUID? — Encyclopedie Annuelle, 1963, Plon, Paris;
dates for Great Britain and Mexico author's estimates.

ABOUT THE AUTHOR

David R. Raynolds spent 1958-61 in El Salvador with the United States Foreign Service. Additional Latin American service in the Dominican Republic helped provide the background for compiling this volume. Mr. Raynolds has served on the staff of the Executive Secretariat of NATO in Paris and with the Policy Planning Council in Washington. His professional experience also includes the management and editing of a magazine and service with a public relations firm.

Mr. Raynolds has published articles and has lectured on American diplomacy and international economics. He was graduated with honors in English from Dartmouth College in 1949 and received an M.A. degree in history from Wesleyan University in 1955. He pursued further graduate work at The Johns Hopkins School of Advanced International Studies and George Washington University.